IN THE PRESENCE
OF A MASTER

GURUDEV
Yogi Amrit Desai

Edited by Christine Deslauriers (Sukanya)

◆ KRIPALU PUBLICATIONS ◆

By Yogi Amrit Desai:

Happiness Is Now
Working Miracles of Love
Kripalu Yoga: Meditation in Motion
Kripalu Yoga: Meditation in Motion, Book II
The Wisdom of the Body
Love Is an Awakening
Loving Each Other
Listen with Your Heart

About Yogi Amrit Desai:

Gurudev: The Life of Yogi Amrit Desai
by Christine Deslauriers (*Sukanya*)

*For information about Kripalu Center,
write P. O. Box 793, Lenox, MA 01240*

Cover photo by Ron King

Kripalu Publications, P. O. Box 793, Lenox, MA 01240
ISBN 0-940258-25-0 (hbk.) ISBN 0-940258-26-9 (pbk.)
Library of Congress Catalog Card Number: 92-72739

This book is dedicated to Gurudev
in grateful appreciation
on his sixtieth birthday.

For seeing the light in us all,
and teaching us to see it,
we celebrate your existence,
your presence
in our lives.

From all your Kripalu family

We gratefully acknowledge the following individuals
whose generous contributions funded the publication of this book:

Dick *(Ananda)* & Franchesca Bertram
Jules & Carol Cohen *(Mahesh & Parvati)*
Lelia Griswold *(Jyotika)*
Barbara Hoffman *(Pranshakti)*
Rex & Denise Inglis *(Priyatam & Priyada)*
Ming Lash *(Kanta)* in loving memory of Eliott *(Kanti)*
Ellyn Lyman *(Renu)*
Doug & Monica Mitchell
Stephan & Eva Slane *(Gopinath & Gitadevi)*
Sonja *(Bhagini)* & Michael Stewart
Peter Strauss
Reinaldo & Arlene Winer *(Devraj & Devaki)*

Foreword

When I realized that it would soon be Gurudev's sixtieth birthday as well as the thirtieth anniversary of the beginning of his teaching in America, it seemed an appropriate time to celebrate the profound impact on the world of his life and work. As part of that celebration I commission-ed the writing of this commemorative book, in order to share with as great a number as possible the transformation that I and thousands of others have experienced through knowing this extraordinary human being and practicing his teachings.

This book is a gift of love from all of us at Kripalu to those of you who feel stirred to the deepest levels of your heart and spirit as you read it. It is more than its collection of stories and teachings; it is an invitation to know Gurudev intimately, through his words and through the eyes of those who have lived and worked closely with him.

This book is also a "thank you" to all of you who over the years have given of your time, skills, enthusiasm, love, and support to contribute to the expanding work of Kripalu and Gurudev.

To Gurudev, through whom my soul has awakened to possibilities far beyond my limited mind, I say:

Some offer to teach how to walk

Others offer instruction in the art of flying

You have given me wings to soar and offered to soar by my side

Sandra Healy (Krishnapriya)
Executive Director, Kripalu Yoga Fellowship

In Appreciation

It was Krishnapriya's visionary love for Gurudev that conceived this book and brought it into existence. Her inspired imagining of the project made it a reality.

Most of the stories about Gurudev were gathered by Bhavani through many interviews. She also contributed her formidable copy editing skills. From over one thousand pages of transcribed material, Aruni crafted the stories with me; she was a joy to write with. With her poetic eye she also edited the meditative verses by Gurudev that appear in this book.

Chandra's outstanding editorial direction refined and streamlined the manuscript. He poured himself into the project and supported the work both creatively and strategically. I also want to acknowledge Chitra, whose continuous, excellent editorial input on the entire manuscript I highly valued.

The tireless efforts of the design team—Narendra and Vikram—gave visual beauty and form to the book. The photographs were drawn from the Kripalu Center's collection and were taken primarily by Prakash, Himanshu, Prembala, Subodh, Niti, Pandavi, Janki, Ramakrishna, Saguna, and Laxmikant.

My husband and partner, Praphul, was a caring and wise supporter throughout the project. His calm ability to see through difficulties to resolution and his insightful presence during my darshans with Gurudev were integral to my work.

Many others, too numerous to mention, gave their time and sincere care to the creation of this tribute to Gurudev. To all of them I extend my deepest thanks.

Christine Deslauriers (Sukanya)
Editor

IN THE PRESENCE OF A MASTER

Preface: Introducing Yogi Amrit Desai

Yogi Amrit Desai, known to his thousands of students and disciples as Gurudev, is the originator of Kripalu Yoga and the founder and spiritual director of Kripalu Center for Yoga and Health in Lenox, Massachusetts. An internationally renowned speaker, seminar leader, and author in the field of yoga and holistic living, he is widely recognized and honored as a spiritual teacher.*

Gurudev was born on October 16, 1932 in a rural town in Gujarat State, India. At the age of sixteen he met his guru, Swami Shri Kripalvanandji (Kripalu), lovingly called "Bapuji" ("dear father") by his many thousands of disciples and revered in India as one of the greatest living masters of Kundalini Yoga. Amrit's spiritual purity and potential, present even at that early age, was recognized by Bapuji and in a short time Amrit became a close disciple.

In 1960, at the age of twenty-eight, Gurudev moved to the United States to study at the Philadelphia College of Art. Attending classes by day, living very frugally, and working the night shift in a factory, he soon saved enough money to bring his wife Urmila (now called "Mataji") and infant son to America.

Gurudev quickly became a recognized and award-winning artist and textile designer. But even while he was creating beautiful art, his true passion—the practice of yoga—was occupying more and more of his time and attention. His visit to India in 1966 for further study with his guru inspired him to devote all his energies to yoga. He left behind his flourishing art career and founded the Yoga Society of Pennsylvania, an organization through which he trained over fifty yoga teachers and which by 1970 was conducting one hundred fifty classes with more than two thousand students each semester.

In 1970, during his routine morning yoga practice, Gurudev was drawn into a profound state of meditation and experienced a spiritual awakening that proved to be a landmark in his inner transformation. As a direct result, Bapuji called Gurudev to India to give him the highest form of shaktipat initiation and to bestow on him the rare and extraordinary power to give shaktipat to deserving spiritual seekers.** After Gurudev's return from India, hundreds of people experienced powerful visions, spontaneous catharsis, and other manifestations of shakti in his presence.

---

* Gurudev's life story and the roots of the Kripalu path have been recounted in two books: *Gurudev: The Life of Yogi Amrit Desai* by Christine Deslauriers (Sukanya) and *Light from Guru to Disciple* by Swami Shri Rajarshi Muni. The latter tells the extraordinary story of Gurudev's guru, Bapuji, and Bapuji's guru, Dadaji.
** For information about shaktipat, see the article on page 84.

Gurudev with his immediate family: (from left to right) Kamini, Malay, Mataji, Gurudev, Amar, Kinnari, Pragnesh.

The noticeably profound shift in his energy and in the impact of his teachings inspired his students to begin calling him "Gurudev," which means "beloved teacher."

Gurudev's spiritual awakening transformed his life and completely changed his approach to yoga, resulting in his development of Kripalu Yoga Meditation In Motion. Kripalu Yoga captures the spirit and depth of ancient yogic teachings, a depth that had been missing from the popular practice of yoga in the West, and at the same time makes yoga accessible to even the busiest of modern spiritual seekers.

In 1972 Gurudev and his family moved from Philadelphia to a property in Sumneytown, Pennsylvania that he purchased for his family's residence and his own deepening spiritual practice. Several of his yoga students asked to live and study there with him and he consented.

Within two years there sprang up around Gurudev a flourishing yoga community, or ashram, consisting of over fifty adults drawn by the power of his teachings and the transforming impact of living in his presence. Gurudev's uncompromising commitment to transformation through a lifestyle of love and service to humanity created the ashram as a place where American disciples could practice the most profound spiritual teachings in their daily lives. In 1976, to accommodate growing numbers of residents and guests, the ashram expanded its services and facilities by acquiring a much larger property at Summit Station, Pennsylvania.

From the beginning Gurudev considered his founding of ashrams, his development of Kripalu Yoga, and all the other forms of his humanitarian service to be an expression of his love for and dedication to Bapuji. That is why it is Swami Kripalu's name rather than his own that emblazons all of Gurudev's work.

In 1977 Bapuji came to the United States to honor his spiritual grandchildren's unceasing requests for his visit. While residing at the Summit Station property he continued his intensive schedule of meditating ten hours a day and, in a rare break in his eighteen years of silence and contemplation, spent many mornings teaching the American disciples about yoga and spiritual living.*

Bapuji later moved to Muktidham, the more secluded meditation retreat cabin at the Sumneytown ashram, and reduced his darshans to a weekly, one-hour silent audience with disciples and guests. His presence was an immense joy and inspiration to all who were fortunate enough to experience the profound spiritual impact of his darshan. Bapuji returned to India in 1981, and entered mahasamadhi a few months later. (In India, the passing of a great spiritual master is called "maha-samadhi," or "great samadhi,"—a final, conscious act of liberation.)

The Kripalu work continued to expand and in 1983 Gurudev established Kripalu Center in Massachusetts, where he remains in residence. The Center has a large pro-

fessional staff and serves over fifteen thousand guests each year. (For more information about Kripalu Center, see the Appendix.)

Over the years Gurudev has been honored repeatedly for his outstanding service to the world and his mastery in the field of yoga. For example, he was awarded the title of Yogacharya ("Spiritual Preceptor") by Swami Kripalvanandji in 1980, the title of Maharishi ("Great Sage") by the highly revered Swami Gangeshvaranandji in 1982, and the title of Jagadacharya ("World Teacher") by the World Religious Parliament in 1986. In 1987 the President of India presented Gurudev with the World Development Council's Vishva Yoga Ratna award, which recognized Gurudev's life-long work in the field of yoga.

As recognition of Gurudev has grown, he has frequently been invited to teach at international conferences held by organizations like the European Yoga Teachers Association, whose annual conference in Zinal, Switzerland is attended by over one thousand yoga teachers. He has been the keynote speaker at the International Conference on Science and Religion in New Delhi, and in 1990 the Soviet Ministry of Health invited him to Moscow to join the Center for Soviet-American Dialogue as one of the leading speakers at the first Soviet-American Conference on Yoga and Meditation.

Today Gurudev's seminars in America, Russia, China, Japan, Europe, Iceland, and elsewhere are touching people throughout the world, resulting in the formation of more than one hundred associated support

*These talks are available in Swami Shri Kripalvanandji's *Premyatra: Pilgrimage of Love, Books I, II, and III.* (Lenox, MA: Kripalu Publications)

groups and centers, with thousands of teachers and tens of thousands of students. The mother center for this worldwide network, Kripalu Center, is a more than twenty-year-old spiritual community—an active ashram of Westerners living the ancient disciplines of yoga. Through all the many expressions of the Kripalu work, Gurudev is practicing the spirit of his guru's universal approach to humanitarian service: *vasudhaiva kutumbakam*—"the world is one family."

Introduction

In the Presence of a Master is a celebration of the spiritual teacher, Yogi Amrit Desai—Gurudev—on his sixtieth birthday. It is an offering of the heart from disciples and friends, an honoring of the tremendous gifts given to us by this unique and wonderful human being who is our guru.

Through the teachings and stories in this book, Gurudev opens up his inner world: he reveals the personal values that direct his life, shares his private feelings about his guru, Bapuji, and illuminates for us the way he handles challenging events. Gurudev illustrates his way of responding to what life brings him, showing us how he converts the experience of human life into a powerful catalyst for transformation. Often citing examples from his life or answering personal questions from seekers, Gurudev creates a relatable context for applying deeper spiritual truths to everyday situations. The disciples' stories of their experiences with Gurudev further illustrate his consciousness, vision, and humanity.

Conceived as our gift to Gurudev, this book was fashioned from the desire to express our gratitude to Gurudev and to celebrate his life. But in the paradox of the guru-disciple relationship, the more the disciple gives to the guru, the more the guru gives back to the disciple. In sharing our guru stories, in crafting the teaching articles, and in taking the photographs to illustrate the book, all of us involved have been reminded of who we truly are, reawakened by Gurudev to a deeper truth, a more open heart, a fuller sense of self. Gurudev, the expansive giver and divine magician, has turned the tables on us once again and made this book *his* offering of love to us.

Gurudev worked extensively on the teachings found in this book, and it was a great honor and joy to work with him in formulating and refining the articles. He is an impeccable writer and cares deeply about every sentence. His profound care stems from his love for the truth and his desire to serve our growth to the maximum through whatever vehicle he is using—in this case, the written word. Even as he poured hours of his most creative morning time into the editing process, he maintained his characteristic nonattachment to the final product.

Here is a snapshot of Gurudev working on this book. He enters his darshan room at eight o'clock in the morning, wearing his favorite well-worn beige velour robe. Gurudev never slumps into a room, even when he has a bad cold or just flew back from China the day before. He strides in with irrepressible anticipation of the creative process. His spirited enthusiasm fills the room and sparkles through the writing, like the morning sunlight that suffuses his darshan room. He has an elegant rosewood

couch but sits on the floor. We use an old Kleenex box to prop up the microphone. His dynamism cascades through the room as the onrush of ideas, inspirations, thoughts, connecting concepts, and brilliant insights flow from him.

When Gurudev suddenly thinks of a book, letter, old journal, or gift someone gave him that relates to our task at hand, he goes immediately upstairs to his study to fetch it for our use. When Gurudev moves, he almost runs, like a teenager. He is so overflowing with prana that he can't just plod along. He flows upstairs, then returns to his floor pillow, adjusting the beige velour folds, pushing his silvery-black hair behind one ear, and adjusting his glasses, utterly unselfconscious.

"Here it is!" he says delightedly, sharing whatever old letter from Bapuji, book from a friend, newspaper clipping, or gift he wanted to bring forth.

Gurudev thinks in terms of potentials, endless possibilities, and boundless "why not?" creativity. To be in his presence infuses you with that same spirit of "Yes, why not?" Everything is possible with Gurudev. No door is shut until you feel it against your nose, and even then Gurudev will find a creative way to open it. He sees the path around the pothole, not the pothole. But while seeing the vast potential of everything, he is also fully accepting of the reality of limits. He doesn't fight.

Expansive by nature, Gurudev thinks inclusively of people to talk to, people to call, people to invite and include in this meeting, that darshan, this project. He respects everyone equally and seems to want everyone to feel needed, drawn on, and called forth in their gifts and abilities. Every book-related darshan was punctuated with his requests: "Ask this one to

write. Call that one for a story. Find out what this one would suggest. Meet with that one for ideas."

Every minute counts with Gurudev. Energy is sacred and there is no waste in his input on the writing. Nearly everything he has to offer in a four-hour writing darshan will have great value and potential to improve the piece we are editing. It is an affectionate joke among the ashram editors that if you take a three-page article to Gurudev for input, you'll walk out with forty pages to transcribe. That occurs because Gurudev sees everything as interconnected.

When Gurudev has an idea—which is about every twenty seconds—his transferable vitality and aliveness spill out into the room. His eyes glow and his voice is animated. One idea generates another, progressively moving deeper and deeper toward some ultimate truth. He can hardly contain his joy and enthusiasm at the unfolding flow of insights and ideas tripping through his mind. He wants to get every idea out, he wants always to help the reader see clearly, learn more, understand better.

Gurudev seems as pleased and surprised at the brilliantly interweaving ideas tumbling out of his mouth as I am. "There! That was it," he'll say with a broad smile—the wonderful smile of his that is so genuine. "It never came out quite like that before!" he'll often exclaim in unstudied delight, as if I had said it, not he. It's as if he were a cosmic radio, listening

in fascination to the messages coming over the airwaves. His pleasure in exploring truth is contagious. All who are exposed catch the joy and walk away uplifted, renewed, changed.

Yet with all that investment and enthusiasm, Gurudev remains absolutely unattached to things happening a certain way. That was illustrated perfectly when, eight months into the project, after Gurudev had spent countless mornings writing with me, it appeared for a time that it might be necessary to cancel the book due to unforeseen staffing difficulties. I was not at all surprised to see Gurudev's complete equanimity with dropping the book that was created to honor and celebrate him, even after his own considerable investment of time.

That is Gurudev—total in whatever he's involved in, yet completely open to what's happening next. He trusts life; he doesn't need to control or direct it. He has an absolute belief that whatever is happening is perfect, and that by responding to it with acceptance and receptivity, everything will unfold according to divine plan. And because he believes it, that is his experience.

Regardless of Gurudev's input on all the teachings found here, the full depth of his message could never be contained in one book, nor expressed fully by someone not yet established in the astounding consciousness he lives from. Whatever incompletions or shortcomings remain in the writing belong entirely to me.

— Christine Deslauriers (Sukanya)

LIFE HAS A PLAN FOR ME

I have no plan for my life.
   I accept the plan life has for me.
I follow that plan, and what it provides me moment
   to moment.
I am not the roles I play in following the plan.
I am the witness of all that I interact with in my life.
I was a child, an adult, and will soon be an old man.
I was a son, a brother, a husband, a father, and a grandfather.
I was an artist, a businessman, a yogi, a guru, a friend.
I have been healthy, sick, successful, a failure, awake,
   and asleep.
Behind all those changing experiences, I am the changeless
   consciousness that is constantly present.
I am that I am, in spite of the changes that "I am" experiences.
I am That.
My present is pregnant with all my past.
My future unfolds from the way I live my present.
My being manifests in the present.
I am present.
I am at home in the eternal now, living the plan life has for me.

In The Center Of The Vortex

Who is Gurudev? Whatever I say confines him and makes him smaller than he really is. Because of the limitations in my seeing, at any one time in my ten years with him I have seen only a tiny piece of who he is. He is immense, beyond my understanding.

Gurudev is like the center of a mandala, where there is a black hole, a creative vortex where anything can happen. He lives in the center of the vortex, willing to create without preconceived ideas. Life presents challenges, and Gurudev bursts forth into creation in response to life.

He is creation with human skin over it.

When I am with Gurudev I have the privilege of resonating with his level of evolution. His presence educates me about who I really am—the integration of humanity and divinity. When I am with him I am on an evolutionary jet ride. He is shakti energy, propelling me forward toward truth. Whatever external events Gurudev creates for me—whether they are projects, programs, or new yoga practices—all are merely excuses for me to travel with him and to grow from my contact with him.

Many masters consider the material world antagonistic to spiritual life; they offer an anti-physical kind of existence spent in secluded meditation, out of contact with human joys and experiences. But Gurudev models how to live in an American, twentieth century time/space and reach for oneness at the same time. He models the integration of the humanity and divinity that exist within us all, and shows how to live at an enlightened vibration while doing human work. He lives a human life as a husband and father, fulfilling the roles prescribed by his dharma. He's willing to feel the human emotions that surface in this life, and yet he has the same spiritual force and desire for truth as a swami living in a cave.

My human business isn't finished. I couldn't have gone to India to meditate; I have too many lessons to resolve here in my world. Being with Gurudev on this path is perfect for me.

On the Kripalu path, you don't need a spiritual Ph.D. before you're allowed to meet the master. You're allowed to study with him while still in nursery school. And this master loves you so much that he comes to nursery school with you and brings you his spiritual teachings on a level you can use, here and now.

To find this living master, you don't have to walk on a secret path found only in the moonlight in the middle of the Amazon. No, he's right here in the middle of New England. He answers his own phone. He shows up with spills on his clothes. He is Mr. Ordinary, yet he is a king, and he teaches you how to behave like spiritual royalty. He shows you the integration of humbleness and regality, the synchronization of the most ordinary and the most spiritual dimensions.

Gurudev doesn't promise me that I'm going to heaven with him, that I've been with him in Egypt or Atlantis, or that we will be together in the future. He offers me none of the fantasies that would hook me. Instead, he teaches me how to live my life, daily. There is no false romanticism about Gurudev. He says, "I'm here to help you connect to your own inner guru. I'm not here for you to get hooked on me and become sheep." Through my discipleship, I have not become Gurudev. Who I've become is myself.

— *SUMITRA*

3

It's Not in the Numbers

Just out of college, I was in Holland, preparing to teach my first Kripalu seminar. I had invested a lot of time and energy into designing and marketing my program. In the beginning, I had felt enthusiastic and confident of success, but as the seminar approached, I started to experience self-doubt and fear.

Despite all my work, only one person had signed up. I interpreted that to mean that I was doing something wrong, and felt progressively more doubtful about my ability to teach. My expectations of myself were heightened by the fact that I happen to be the daughter of the best of all seminar leaders, Gurudev.

A few days before the seminar was to begin, my dad called me. He said, "How are you doing? How is the seminar going?"

I burst into tears. "Dad, I'm afraid you are going to think I'm a failure. Not many people have signed up for the seminar. I feel terrible—I feel that I've let you down."

"It doesn't matter how many people are there," he said. I held the phone tight against my ear, straining to hear his loving response. "All that matters is the love you bring to them. Give all of yourself, whether to one person or to six hundred. Even if only one person attends, if that person feels loved, you are a success."

I sighed with relief and relaxed my grip on the telephone.

"I have been in similar circumstances," he continued. "When I left Philadelphia and bought the Sumneytown property in the country, I had only four people with me. That was the beginning of the ashram—four people. In addition, I had a wife, two sons, and you, my young daughter. I didn't know what would happen, but I went where my life was taking me. The externals didn't matter. My faith allowed me to trust my experience. So be fully present and trust your internal knowing, whether the external situation involves four people or four thousand."

That conversation was a gift to me. When I hung up, I felt energized and ready for whatever the seminar might offer.

Six people attended the program. As we did Kripalu Yoga and studied basic yogic teachings, I felt completely engaged with them and enjoyed the process of sharing and teaching. At the end of the seminar, one of the participants came over to speak with me. "Thank you so much," she said, smiling. "These days have been wonderful for me. You're so caring. I've received the essence of Kripalu through your love."

— *KAMINI*

GURUDEV'S VALUES FOR LIVING

The purpose for which I was born is transformation—the removal from my consciousness of every limiting concept, emotional block, or thought that separates me from my true self and therefore from God.

As we transform we become more and more able to release automatically the concepts that block greater consciousness. Consciousness is like the light on a miner's hat: it throws its light wherever we turn, illuminating everything and everyone with the radiance of reality. As we see what is, we start to let go of false ideas of what *should be* and free ourselves from the suffering caused by the discrepancy between reality and our expectations about reality.

My Inner Values Direct My Outer Expression

From my childhood I've always sought a lifestyle that would provide the greatest potential for my transformation. My actions, directed by my inner values of growth and consciousness, are a vehicle for that transformation. Everything I do is intimately connected to my purpose for living.

Kripalu Center, the disciples, and all the external manifestations of the Kripalu work are my *karma bhumi*: the field of action through which I constantly attune myself inwardly and do my inner work. I have not forced or willed any of my external achievements to happen; rather, they have all occurred naturally as I followed my inner longing for transformation. I have simply responded to what presented itself to me, day by day, and used every situation for my growth. As I have done that, Kripalu has grown and flourished organically.

In my heart I know I am not the doer of the Kripalu work. I've never had a goal to create ashrams and centers and draw many disciples to me; nor have I felt a sense of responsibility or excitement when those showed up in my life. I have never thought "Now my dreams have come true," because I've had no dreams. My purpose has been only to live for the inner values that sustain my spirit and the consciousness my soul yearns to express.

It's not that I don't make plans or take actions that support Kripalu's work; I do both. But I never let my plans become dreams.

Any dream of achieving something external would attach me to trying to force things to happen a certain way. I would then feel nervous, controlling, and fearful in carrying out my external work. My fearful, ego-driven consciousness would be felt by my disciples, work its

The Shadow Saint

In Hindu mythology there is a story about a Shadow Saint that reminds me of Gurudev. A great spiritual seeker was visited by Lord Shiva as a reward for the sincerity of his devotion. Shiva said to his devotee, "I will grant you any boon." The devotee said, "I can accept, Lord, only if you grant me both of the following wishes."

The seeker, dizzy with the ecstasy of being with his Lord, said, "The first thing that I ask for, Shiva, is that you bless my shadow. If my shadow touches someone who is sick, let that person become well. If my shadow touches someone who is poor, grant that person wealth. If my shadow touches a seeker of God, grace the seeker with knowing. No matter where my shadow falls, your blessings, dear Shiva, will be showered on every being."

Shiva, proud of his disciple's selflessness, agreed to that. He asked the devotee for his second request, which he assumed would be more personal.

"Dear Shiva," the seeker said, "I will accept the first boon only if you also bless me such that my face will always face the sun. In that way I will never see the works that my shadow is doing."

In the early days of the ashram, there was a sister who had a severe fungus condition on her hand. It was broken-out, raw, and rough looking. One day Gurudev happened to meet her on the walkway. He innocently took her hand and walked with her a while. The next day there wasn't a mark on her hand. It was completely restored to normal appearance.

Gurudev didn't have to say, "Come here, sister. I love you. I'll walk with you and heal you." I don't think he even knew he was doing anything. Nothing was said; no claims were made. He exists at that level of purity.

— *MICKEY SINGER*

expansion of consciousness. My outer work and inner transformation thus complement and support each other.

My disciples are my sadhana. In teaching them I learn; in helping them I receive help; in loving them I receive love. Helping others awaken is the vehicle that stimulates my own awakening.

The problems and challenges that arise within the ashram are an asset to my sadhana when I work with them consciously. They invite me to see my limitations and break through my inner barriers. As I learn to let go, every problem becomes an opportunity to drop my pride, ego, and limitations.

It may appear that I am here to teach others; only a few can see that I am really here to learn. Teaching is secondary. Teaching is about letting go of what I've learned, rather than acquiring new learning. Letting go *is* learning.

way into their behavior, and be reflected through the Center's programs, services, and vibration. The guests would receive that energy and ultimately it would return to me. So I focus my attention not on achieving some dream, but on transforming myself.

My Disciples Are My Sadhana

I have chosen to work intimately with disciples and others who seek transformation as I do. That choice places me in situations that foster my growth while I serve the growth of others, because serving draws the best out of me and keeps me immersed in matters concerning the

I Am A Disciple

It may appear that I am a guru but in my heart I am a disciple—a disciple of life as well as of Bapuji. If I stopped being a disciple I could not be a guru.

The essence of the guru-disciple relationship is transformation, not only for the disciple but for the guru as well. I want my disciples to know that I am not perfect; like them, I am practicing. Being a guru

I have come not to teach you, but to love you. The love will teach you.

–Gurudev

is a way to practice being a disciple.

My spirit of discipleship makes transformation possible for those I am teaching. As we both recognize that we are playing roles to promote our mutual transformation, the energetic transmission of the deeper teachings becomes possible.

In the early days my concepts about being a guru and having disciples were constantly challenged by the living, present relationship between me and those who came to me as spiritual seekers. I saw quickly that to use the guru-disciple relationship for my transformation as well as that of my disciples, I had to let go of the role as I had conceived it.

In teaching and serving my disciples, I practiced letting reality take over and allowing my concepts to disintegrate. Every thought I had about being a guru had to

go. I had to put behind me my fears and attachments, my desires and priorities, my Eastern cultural values and social conditioning, and my ideas of guru and disciple. I had to drop all my images about what a guru is and how a guru should act. Only in the empty space beyond concepts could I attune to my purpose in life and let my inner guidance direct my actions.

There is no dropping of concepts about your role in a relationship without dropping your concepts of the other's role too. So I had to release all my expectations and conditioning about the way my disciples should behave. I had to let go of thinking they should behave toward their guru in the traditional Eastern sense: always doing what the guru asked and never challenging the guru or processing personal emotions with him.

The Master's Offering

In 1990, a group of ashram residents who have taken lifetime vows of renunciation embarked on a pilgrimage to holy places throughout India. Gurudev led us on this spiritual journey.

For me, the most profound part of the pilgrimage was our visit to Kayavarohan, the site of a magnificent temple that houses a statue of Bapuji's guru, lovingly referred to by Kripalu disciples as "Dadaji." It was to greet and honor this image of the preceptor of our lineage that we had traveled thousands of miles to India.

We spent an entire day in the temple, as one powerful ceremony followed another. Many Indian devotees were present also, to welcome the American disciples and to invite us to participate in the worship of Dadaji.

The culmination of the day was arati, a striking ceremony of light. As the pujari waved the lamps of burning oil lovingly before Dadaji's statue in the ancient pattern of arati, we all watched, spellbound by the lights flickering across Dadaji's face. We were drawn deeply into this moment that we had dreamed about for years.

In India, the arati lights are offered first to the gods and the guru, and then to honored guests. When it came time for the pujari to offer the light to Gurudev, instead of receiving it first and acknowledging himself as the center of importance, Gurudev gently guided the hands of the pujari toward us, his disciples. Through his body language, he directed the pujari to offer the light to us first. With great joy, we received the sacred arati light in the temple of Kayavarohan.

Following the ceremony of lights, the tray of blessed food called prasad was passed for each person to partake of. As with the light, Gurudev made sure that we received the prasad first. Even before our guru, we received the blessings of Dadaji—blessings for which we had waited a lifetime.

Gurudev is never concerned with securing or enhancing his own stature or importance. Instead, his focus is on acknowledging everyone who is present and seeing that they receive. He is there almost as an absence, an opening to pass on whatever honors or attention are being paid to him.

He holds his responsibility to nurture the spiritual growth of his disciples as his dharma, his personal duty.

Through his simple gestures on that day, Gurudev's commitment to us was made clear. What he did appeared so simple. He offered us the arati light; he offered us prasad.

Yet there was nothing at all simple about it. His gestures were a statement of the priority he gives to us and our souls' yearnings. We received far more than the blessings of light and prasad that day. With them, we received Gurudev's love and his commitment to us.

— *BRAHMANAND*

11

My American disciples had no concepts about the guru-disciple relationship; they developed their own expression of discipleship. If I had held to my original expectations of them, my need for them to fulfill those expectations would have dominated my thinking and kept me from living in reality. I would have blocked the flow of spirit between us and kept the transmission of energy and consciousness from happening at a deep and subtle level.

I honor reality. Reality is more sacred to me than my most sacred concepts. By releasing my expectations of my disciples I embraced the reality of who they were and thus deepened both my transformative process and my ability to serve theirs.

The main block to transformation is the thought that we shouldn't be where we are, that we should already be farther along in our growth than we perceive ourselves to be. I love my disciples for who they are right now in their human journey.

As I embrace my disciples' reality, something unique happens: in feeling loved for who they are, they have the opportunity to drop any need to deny themselves or show up differently. They

> *I honor reality. Reality is more sacred to me than my most sacred concepts... Reality is the messenger of consciousness. I want to see reality; I don't want to hide from it.*

learn to accept where they are in their growth right now. That self-acceptance then moves them forward, my acceptance of them having served as a catalyst for their transformation.

I don't focus on accepting others; in my heart I focus on accepting the reality they represent to me. I'm loving reality through them: reality is God in disguise. I love God through each person I meet. But others may experience my recognition of God in them as my loving and accepting them personally. And feeling loved, they are able to come closer to their divine, true self through our interaction.

Be careful not to get stuck in the subtle trap of accepting others so you can reinforce your ego and congratulate yourself for being accepting. The idea is not to accept individuals, but to accept what life is presenting to you *through* them. By making that shift in consciousness, you create an opening for others to accept reality and be transformed too.

Such acceptance of reality is what we really mean by the word "love." Love is just accepting reality. It is not necessarily an emotional experience; it is impersonal and universal.

12

"I'm Like Me"

[Note: Unlike today, in the early 1970's most Kripalu residents were "renunciates," single people in their twenties who formally gave up their worldly goods, practiced celibacy, and lived a simple, almost monastic lifestyle.]

Once in 1974 I was sharing with Gurudev about some emotional issues that were coming up for me.

"Gurudev," I said, "I'm not like everyone else at the ashram. I'm married. It's hard for me to follow guidelines like brahmacharya. Most residents are young and have few worldly goods. I'm thirty years old, I have some financial assets, and I'm not sure how I want to use them. And Gurudev," I added, "I don't really know that I want to be just like you. I want a relationship with my wife that is different from the purely spiritual one you have with Mataji. I'm not sure this is the right path for me. Am I a second-rate disciple?"

Gurudev was quiet during my entire monologue. Then he leaned close to me with a big grin. He said, "I'm not anything like Bapuji. Bapuji has no hair and I have really long hair. Bapuji's not married and I have a wife and three children. Bapuji doesn't own anything and I do. I'm not anything like Bapuji. I'm like me."

I stopped. I listened. I really heard that I didn't have to be like Gurudev. I heard that as much as Gurudev loved and emulated Bapuji, all he cared to be was the best Amrit Desai he could be. He wasn't trying to be Bapuji; he was being Amrit Desai.

So I learned to be the best Shankar. My mantra became, "I am who I am, and I'm not trying to be like anybody else." Gurudev helped me let go of my feelings of being a second-rate disciple and love myself for who I am.

— *SHANKAR*

Not Your Usual Leader

An international consultant to Fortune 500 CEO's and heads of governments, I arrived at Kripalu ready to relax and slow down. I had no idea what I was coming to. I thought it was going to be a yoga version of Club Med. What a surprise Kripalu was, and the biggest surprise came when I got to know its founder and spiritual leader, Gurudev.

I was asked to become a consultant to Kripalu Yoga Fellowship, and over two years I observed Gurudev at close range. We became friends and spent many hours in tête à tête discussions. My conclusion is that of the many powerful and distinguished leaders I have encountered, Gurudev is unique. He is not your usual leader.

What struck me first was the total absence of ego. There we were dissecting in minute detail the organization he founded and cherishes, yet at no time did he try to push or force his opinion. He had total, absolute trust and faith that the right decisions would be made. He got everything by asking for nothing. What a difference from almost anyone else I have ever known!

Another unique characteristic of Gurudev is his unconditional love. By this I do not mean he agrees with everything and everybody, but for Gurudev disagreement never leads to judging the other person. With Gurudev you always feel that you have absolute room to maneuver; no one is ever cornered or forced to agree on anything. Total empowerment. And this type of behavior is contagious. The disciples all look as if they have Gurudev's eyes—all shining with warmth and acceptance and endless love.

Gurudev's love is not accompanied by a need to be accepted in return. His is an unconditional love, the kind one experiences only as a child, mostly from one's mother. Such love gives so much energy, and it creates a tremendous desire to reciprocate.

What seemed most unusual to me was that Gurudev had chosen to live in the ashram, next to his disciples. I was surprised, because few can survive a twenty-four-hour-a-day examination by dedicated disciples. How can one set an example twenty-four hours a day, three hundred sixty-five days a year? It must create incredible pressure, I thought, to be so transparent and at the same time good enough to be continuously viewed as a model for emulation. Who is that perfect?

After two years of observing Gurudev, I got the answer. He is not trying to be perfect. If he tried, he would fail. What we see is what he is. He is just himself, without trying. This person is real.

There is no end to what I have learned from Gurudev's writings. But I have learned more by observing him; I have learned to accept life, have faith, and be myself.

— ICHAK ADIZES

I Provide The Map; It's Up To Disciples To Travel

I see my disciples as evolving beings needing to learn lessons from their choices and from the experiences that result. My disciples' lives are theirs. They need to learn to make choices based on what they feel guided to do from within themselves. It is my responsibility to provide my disciples with a map; it is up to them to travel.

Sometimes when I see them not following the map I've provided through my life and teachings, my heart hurts at first, because I see in each of them the untapped potential for happiness and peace. But my hurt is not permanent and it is diminishing as my clarity grows. A long time ago I discovered that forcing spiritual teachings on others never works. Knowing that,

I usually give advice only if a disciple asks me for guidance. It's not that I'm uninterested in my disciples' lives; I have great compassion for them. I know, however, that they must learn to take responsibility for themselves.

Letting My Ego Die While I'm Alive

Kripalu is not my work; it is God's work. I consider the extraordinary growth of the Kripalu work and the difference it has made in others' lives to be the grace of God and guru. I initiated the work but I am not the conductor or achiever of it. Knowing that gives me the capacity to serve people without judging them or needing to control them. In my heart I offer the results of my service to God, saying "Thy will be done, not mine. My share is to do this work. It is your part

to direct the work in whatever way you choose." The results of my service are then out of my hands and I am free.

The work of Kripalu is the mirror in which I see myself and face whatever I need to. I experience Kripalu as a here and now phenomenon in my life, not a product to be guaranteed into the future. I want to face right now, while I am here on this earth, everything that could happen in the organization after I have left my body. I want to see it all so I can use it as an opportunity to drop my ego. I want my ego to die before my body dies. If I can die to my ego, if I can let anything happen in front of me here and now with acceptance rather than resistance, I will find the transformation I long for and fulfill my purpose in being on this planet.

Reality is the messenger of consciousness. I want to see reality; I don't want to hide from it. If there will be among my disciples the sort of factions that often develop after a guru dies, I want to be able to respond to that consciously in this life and accept it without blaming anyone or feeling guilty. I am willing to face that possibility, not because I want it to occur, but because it presents another opportunity for my transformation. And if the Kripalu organization falls apart the moment I die, what's the difference? Everything was moving along in this world before I was born; after I die it will continue without me. I am not keeping it all together.

I Want To Be Nobody

I want to be nobody. As I progressively move toward death I know I have less and less under my control for the future. When I die, everything that has been manifested in the Kripalu work will be out of my control. For me, the path of consciousness is to let go before it is all taken away from me. My preparation for death is to live consciously now.

If one day I awake and realize I need a different setting to follow truthfully my primary intention of growth, I will make that change. If I come to a stage where I need to go into seclusion, for example, I will take that as the next action in alignment with my primary purpose. My seclusion or leaving the ashram would not mean I was tired or frustrated with my disciples or the organization. It would be a moving *toward* what my soul yearns for rather than an escaping *from* what my ego is resisting.

I want my disciples to know how I am making my choices, so they can use my example as a guide for their own choices. This writing that reveals how I live will be available forever for them to reflect on.

By following my intention, I have naturally attracted people who share it. They have come to view me as their guru, I have taught them to use seva for inner unfoldment, and all the Kripalu work has resulted. But in my heart, I'm not looking for anything from anyone. I only want to fulfill the purpose for which I was born: transformation, the return to my true self that exists in the reality beyond my concepts. That is my heart's longing and my mission in life. ◆

Beyond Images

Who is Gurudev anyway? I've been a disciple for twelve years and I'm still asking the question. As far as I can tell, gurus are the ultimate mystery, and Gurudev is no exception.

Over the years he's been the object of my devotion as well as my resistance. He's reassured me with the kindness of a gentle mother and pierced my sense of identity with his direct and unadorned insight. When I've demanded that he meet my expectations, generally he hasn't. And of course when I've least expected it, he's been there for me in ways I couldn't have imagined.

Only now do I begin to see that every statement I make about him says far more about me than about him. The truth just may be that what Gurudev is ultimately about is showing me to me. How else would I become free? How else would I ever get beyond the images and conditioning I call me, and know myself to be something far grander?

For a long time I let the maverick streak in me calcify into something of a rebel image. I actually nurtured it. Eventually I found myself in a small darshan with Gurudev for residents who were questioning ashram guidelines or values. For nearly four hours, Gurudev opened his heart and offered encouragement and inspiration to those of us whose fear, doubt, or anger blocked our ability to participate fully in the ashram lifestyle.

At some point during his sharing, I looked at him. I really looked at him and listened. Finally I said in a quiet voice, "Gurudev, thank you for not giving up on me. Thank you for looking past my image and continuing to believe in me." He turned to face me, his eyes at once soft and penetrating. "I always will believe in you, Kalindi," he said, "I always will."

— *KALINDI*

GURUDEV'S CHILDHOOD DECISION

Very early in my life, I saw that what weighed me down and disturbed my peace of mind the most was blaming someone else for my unhappiness. I saw that blame agitated me, and distracted me from my highest purpose—my personal growth. As soon as I realized that, I decided never to hold onto blame or malice in my heart, no matter what others did. I never wanted to do anything that would disturb my contented heart, because then I could not grow. And to me, even as a child, my growth was everything.

Affirmations

In 1986 I visited my grandmother's house in India with Gurudev, who is my dad. Even though my grandmother had passed on some time before, a lot of Dad's childhood belongings were still stored in her house, the house he grew up in.

I found an early diary of my dad's, a little brown book with yellowed pages. Every page was filled from top to bottom, with no margins. In his beautiful handwriting, Dad had written positive affirmations and quotations over and over again throughout the book. I sat on the floor in my grandmother's house, touched by the vision of my father as a child, writing and rewriting his positive affirmations.

At the time of Dad's childhood, nobody had heard of affirmations, especially in India. He just naturally did them. I saw how the truths expressed in that diary—affirmations of his positive qualities, truths about self-empowerment and self-improvement—have affected his whole life. I saw that my dad was as a young boy the same as he is today: totally committed to growing spiritually and developing all his potential.

— MALAY

Gurudev's Other Guru

Of all the characteristics of Gurudev that I have come to treasure, I most value his openness and willingness to share himself and his life. When I was studying yoga in India, Gurudev welcomed me into his home there at a time of great challenge for him and his family: his mother, a strong and vibrant woman, was on her deathbed.

Gurudev asked me to speak to her and comfort her. I felt highly unqualified for the task, but as usual Gurudev's love empowered me to serve fearlessly, even in the face of death and my own feeling of inadequacy.

I also felt honored, awestruck, and grateful to be in that delicate position. I reached out to Gurudev's mother and told her about the ways he had touched and transformed my life and the lives of thousands of others. She seemed happy that I was being blessed by her son's love, the love she knew so well.

After Gurudev's mother passed away, I shared with him an intuition I had that she might be reincarnated as one of his disciples. Gurudev replied, "I could never be her guru; she will always be my guru—in this life or any other."

— *HARI SHARANA*

MOTHER AND CHILD

See a child
inside mother's womb.

Child has nothing
to do.

Mother provides all.

Child breathes
mother's breath.

Child feeds
from mother's food.

You are in the womb
of the cosmic Mother,
divine Shakti.

Live in ultimate
oneness with her.

Receive all her gifts.

Mother does it all
for you.

You do not even
have to grow.

Mother takes care
of that.

*Trust that everything
you strive for
will be taken care of
in the absence of
your fighting,
your worrying.*

*Feel the warmth
of the Mother.*

*Feel the warmth
of her Love.*

IN THE MOMENT

*I*f you want to experience the joyous ecstasy that life offers, there is one commitment that is absolutely fundamental: the commitment to live in the moment. With that commitment as your guiding focus, whatever you do in your daily life is part of your transformational process. Your commitment to living in the moment becomes your vehicle for spiritual growth.

You are a potential about to happen. You are a possibility in disguise, perpetually being revealed. When you commit to live every moment consciously, you activate your latent spiritual potential. Your commitment to the moment is the driving force actualizing your hidden potentials that are waiting to spring forth. You need do nothing else but be present in each moment. With that one simple practice, you generate your transformation.

Living in the moment, however, is the most dangerous situation anybody ever faces in life, because everything you have ever avoided is revealed to you when you live in the moment. You get to face all the denied contents of your subconscious as they reappear again and again through the events of your life.

When they reappear, you will be frightened. You'll instinctively want to jump into your built-in escape system to repress, avoid, or deny them—to do anything but be with your feelings in receptivity and openness. Remember that the denied material of your subconscious represents all the pain and fear you have not faced in your life. To accept the resurfacing of those feelings is not a simple action.

The only power that can carry you through the reappearance of your denied feelings and fears is a solid commitment to

Into The Dance

In 1982 I was in Alaska running a consulting firm that worked with major oil companies. My professional and financial responsibilities were large and sometimes I felt a lot of pressure.

During that time, Gurudev, accompanied by Mataji, came to give a seminar in Anchorage. After the seminar, Gurudev, Mataji, and a few Alaskan disciples went on a tour above the Arctic Circle to visit some Inuit villages.

We took a plane to the region, then joined two busloads of tourists. Gurudev, the masterful spiritual teacher who had given a powerful seminar only the day before, transformed into a ten-year-old boy, awed by everything around him. He stuck his head out of the bus window, looking at everything with fascination. As we panned for gold and explored the tundra, Gurudev approached every minute with relish.

One night we went to an excellent demonstration of Inuit dancing. The drums were pounding and Gurudev was rapturously engaged. Near the end of the demonstration, the announcer asked, "Who'd like to come down here and join our dance?"

Without a moment's pause, Gurudev thrust his camera into my hands and jumped up, saying to me, "Take my picture! Take my picture!" He took Mataji's arm and moved down the aisle, she shyly resisting every inch of the way by clinging to one of the sisters who was traveling with us. The three of them proceeded toward the stage, the only people out of the group of two hundred to volunteer. As the dancers showed them how to do the intricate steps, Gurudev watched intently.

Before I knew it, Gurudev was bouncing up and down, as free as a child, thoroughly enjoying every beat of the drum. I saw, and captured with his camera, his full expression of total joy, free of any concept or self-image.

Throughout the rest of the tour, Gurudev continued to be fascinated with every experience. He showed me that I can dive into the full experience and expression of each moment if I am not locked into any image or concept of who I think I am. Gurudev modeled the freedom of being open to the wonderment, joy, and mystery of life, ever unfolding.

My Arctic play with Gurudev left a deep impression on me. As Gurudev demonstrated the possibilities of freedom, he reminded me to let go of the weight of the world and jump wholly into life's dance.

— *PRAPHUL*

Living in the moment is the most dangerous situation anybody ever faces in life, because everything you have ever avoided is revealed to you when you live in the moment.

allow them to be present and to experience them fully. Your commitment to live in the moment gives you courage and acceptance to go through the transformative process. Without such a commitment, your mind will construct every reason why you shouldn't face what your subconscious is presenting to you and will create every possible escape.

Commitment enables you to bypass all your fears, mental escapes, and justifications, so that you can face whatever you are experiencing in the moment. It prevents the obstacles and avoidances, which always show up in the journey of self-discovery, from dragging you off your path.

The commitment I am speaking of means that no matter what comes up for you, no matter how you feel, no matter what situations present themselves to you, your commitment to live in the moment guides every action you take. When you commit to your inner growth, you know what course of action to take and what direction to head. You choose your course

of action to align with your urge to grow and evolve.

Once you make that kind of commitment, every choice you make becomes a choice that either supports your commitment to grow or doesn't support it. It's that simple. I'm not speaking of external choices so much as an internal attitude: a decision to be with, rather than avoid, yourself. Your commitment to live in the moment guides the way you encounter everything in your life.

To live fully in the moment, be one hundred percent total in whatever you do, including all the consequences that result. Embrace every moment exactly as it manifests. In so doing, you liberate yourself from your fears and fantasies of the future and the specters of the past, and throw your energies totally into whatever you are

doing *now*. Engage yourself into each moment's activity as fully as if it were the most desirable and pleasurable activity you could wish for. Completely commit yourself to the activity you are doing in that moment.

The way most people live, "moment" and "experience" are two different things. By the word "moment," I am referring to reality. The word "experience" refers to what you are perceiving and feeling in that moment of reality. Between reality and your experience is usually a thick fog of your concepts, beliefs, suppressed fears, undigested feelings, and projections.

When you look at the sky on a cloudy day and describe it, you might say, "The sky is gray, cloudy, and dull." In reality the sky is full of sunlight and space, but the

clouds conceal the true sky from showing forth, and your experience is that of a cloudy day.

It is the same with the events of your life. Most of the time you are not seeing reality, but the thick fog of your denied past, which obscures the truth. The anti-dote to perceiving events through the fog of your past is living in the moment, which reveals the fog for what it is— a mist, covering the true sky.

To live consciously in the moment, you need an unbiased acceptance of reality as it is manifesting right now. You must deeply trust the forces of the universe, and trust yourself. You trust that whatever comes out of a moment will be acceptable to you, because your emphasis is on living in the moment, rather than achieving a

30

Cricket

I was in India with my dad [Gurudev] in 1986. It was a wonderful time for me, filled with opportunities to be with my dad in a different setting and see him in different ways.

One day we were sitting outside my grandmother's house in the village of Halol when Dad saw a group of young boys playing cricket. He got very excited and quickly put on his sneakers and T-shirt, more like an eager ten-year-old boy than a dignified fifty-four-year-old guru. He said to me, "Come on, Malay! Are you coming?"

With that, he ran across a field and jumped over a fence to get to the cricket game. I held back and walked slowly across the field, feeling uncomfortable. We didn't even know these kids. I watched the little boy inside my father come alive as he ran right up to the kids and asked if he could play in their game.

In India this was surprising behavior for a grown man and the kids weren't sure what to make of it. Then they got interested in the game and in having Dad play. They gave him the bat and he began hitting the ball, running back and forth, yelling, and having a great time. I finally dropped my hesitation and joined them for the rest of the noisy, exciting game.

Again and again I have seen Dad jump into life enthusiastically. Because he has no concern for the way people may perceive him or judge him, he is free to participate fully. He is a model for me, reminding me to drop my fear of people's judgement and involve myself totally in all that life offers.

— MALAY

certain external result.

Trust allows you to experience fully, to receive experience without needing to know the outcome of it or be in control of it. Without trust, you live with brakes on, always anticipating something negative and bracing yourself inwardly against that possibility. Your life is consumed with fear, doubt, and hesitation. Trust is the antidote to fear. It allows you to live fully in the moment, without worrying about the consequences to come.

When you live the way I am describing, there is not a single experience that you ever encounter in life that is excluded from your commitment to living fully in the moment. To live that way means living fully in your humanity. Whatever you are doing, you are absolutely total. If you do business, you live your business fully. If you are in relationship, you live your relationship fully. No expressions of life are excluded—absolutely none. Living in the world does not limit your being in

Muddy Puppies

Gurudev has an innate love for anything spontaneous and pure. One beautiful, soft spring day I was photographing him in his backyard for one of our publications. Gurudev was seated on a small tree stump wearing an elegant, full-length white robe and we were discussing the background of the photograph. As an artist and a photographer, Gurudev has a deep sensitivity for composition, lighting, and symmetry.

Suddenly two large, bouncy Alaskan Husky puppies raced around the corner of the house and threw themselves with great abandon, muddy feet first, into Gurudev's lap. Gurudev roared with delight and embraced their wriggling bodies as if they were long lost friends.

"What is proper guru-etiquette for the disciple," I wondered, "when two muddy puppies hurl themselves at the guru?" Having not the faintest idea what to do, I continued photographing while Gurudev wrestled with the pups, becoming covered with multi-patterned paw prints.

A few moments later the puppies leapt off his lap and raced through the open door of his house, tore around in circles on the cream colored carpet, creating another display of paw-print patterns, and then escaped to the mysterious realm from which they had come.

Throughout this frenzy of activity Gurudev completely enjoyed himself. Never once was there a word of regret for the robe, the carpet, or the interrupted session. In the presence of two playful puppies, the elegant spiritual master instantly became a child having a wonderful time.

— *PANDAVI*

the moment; nor does your marriage or your line of work. Nothing external inhibits your spiritual growth or slows down your transformation.

There have been many masters who lived in the world, yet lived in a very high state of consciousness. Sufi masters often worked regular jobs. The magnificent poet-sage Kabir was a carpet weaver. Swami Yogananda's guru, Lahiri Mahasaya, worked as a station master. Jesus was a carpenter.

The consciousness with which those masters acted distinguished their awakened state of being from an ordinary consciousness. On the surface, they looked like ordinary men, but they lived in a different dimension, free from mental dramas. They evidenced their consciousness not through their external activities, but through the presence with which they performed them. They knew that enlightenment occurs through the undivided presence with which each moment is welcomed.

When we make a commitment to live in the moment, we often make the mistake of applying our old concepts about success and failure to the new way of being. Realize that when you start living your commitment, you will occasionally fail and fall; you will get disappointed and frustrated. But that experience of failure will have nothing to do with the way you used to fall and get frustrated. Now the strength of your commitment to living in the moment will pick you up again.

Commitment creates a new space within you, in which you can live unencumbered by your past. That is tremendously liberating. No longer do you have to modify your present experience according

Be one hundred percent total in whatever you do, including all the consequences that result. Embrace every moment exactly as it manifests… Engage yourself into each moment's activity as fully as if it were the most desirable and pleasurable activity you could wish for.

to your past conclusions and concepts. Your commitment brings you a willingness to experience freedom from your past, without any sense of loss or insecurity. It gives you a willingness to move from the known to the unknown. It removes all doubt and hesitation, and plunges you into a passionate involvement with life, exactly as life presents itself to you.

We are constantly modifying and maneuvering our experience and trying to adjust the moment to be more pleasing to us. We have a false concept that the experience we're having is not the right one, so we try to manipulate the moment rather than alter our attitude. Not having lived a given experience completely, we are again and again driven by a desire to experience it fully. Living in the moment means that we do not have to relive a past experience or crave for its repetition.

Amplifying our external experience in the hope it will command our full participation is useless. We instinctively realize we are missing totality. When we mistakenly try to make our external experience more attractive, so that it will engage our complete attention, we're on the wrong track. Experience does not need modification; it needs only to be lived fully. The ecstasy of total involvement comes not from manipulating our external experience, but from being fully in the experience we're having, just the way it is.

Our undigested, painful past experiences also pull our attention away from the present moment. When we struggle to release ourselves from the bondage of the past, we fantasize about having a better future. Instead of embracing the moment that is actually happening, we create a future drama to bail ourselves out of our pain. By living in the moment, we cease to be ruled by the past, and cease living in reaction to our false projections about our past and false promises of future happiness. We exist only in *now*.

Even with a commitment to the moment, your personality can continue to work actively through each of your experiences. Accept your personality; do not try to get rid of anything about yourself. As you live more and more in the moment,

34

Commitment

At Gurudev's suggestion several years ago, many residents made a commitment to daily, early morning practice of Kripalu Yoga for a year and a quarter. At our New Year's celebration the following year, Gurudev taught about the importance of commitment.

He asked the packed room, "How many of you fulfilled your sadhana commitment perfectly this past year and a quarter?"

A small group jumped to their feet and were applauded by Gurudev and the rest of us.

Then he asked, "How many of you did not fulfill your commitment perfectly, but did some sadhana?"

Many people in the room stood up and, to my surprise, so did Gurudev. Everyone began laughing and he, with a tiny smile, said, "Oh, I'm just adjusting my robe." More laughter filled the room.

He said, "I want you all to let go of any illusions about my being perfect, as well as any need you feel to be perfect yourselves." I sat before him, both moved and delighted at his lighthearted humanness.

Gurudev did not have to stand up. He could have sat there, teaching about commitment, allowing us to reject ourselves as we made assumptions about his perfection. But that's not the way he is. He wanted us to know that we are all human and we are all in our humanity together.

Gurudev continued, "I'm grateful that I did as much yoga as I did. If I did not have my commitment to guide me, I would not have practiced yoga as frequently as I did."

By saying that, he gave everyone an opportunity to acknowledge the powerful effects of commitment and to create a successful experience out of what could have been viewed as failure.

Gurudev taught me that day to use commitment as my goal and self-acceptance as my guide.

— *CHIDANAND*

Equanimity

As long as I've known Gurudev, I have found him both an excellent host and a gracious guest. For example, in 1974 he visited the yoga center I was directing in Virginia Beach. In the course of his stay, we offered him widely varying accommodations, yet he seemed comfortable regardless of the external setting.

One night Gurudev stayed in our shabby communal sleeping quarters in a former church rectory with ten yoga students. The following night he was at our sponsor's luxurious lakeside house, with its tennis courts and magnificent view. In each situation I observed Gurudev to be completely at ease, enjoying himself fully.

I witnessed Gurudev's equanimity again when I traveled to India with him in both 1974 and 1986. On the first trip, I and a small group of disciples stayed with Gurudev in Bombay in the ramshackle dormitories of the Salvation Army. Twelve years later, he was no more and no less relaxed and comfortable staying with our tour group at the Taj Mahal Hotel, the pinnacle of luxury and class. Wherever he stayed, Gurudev was grounded in simplicity and unpretentiousness.

Gurudev's flexibility showed up frequently during our 1974 trip, which took place in the midst of a sudden railway strike. Undaunted, Gurudev arranged for us to travel from Bombay to Baroda on an all-night touring bus. The bus had Indian film music blaring continuously over loudspeakers.

At first I was bothered by the fact that I couldn't sleep because of the unending music, but Gurudev pointed out how lucky we were to be able to travel at all under the circumstances. None of us slept aboard the bouncing, boisterous bus, yet Gurudev remained fresh and lively throughout the journey.

Somehow Gurudev's presence could convert even the most unlikely environment into a portable ashram. When we finally arrived in Baroda at dawn after our all-night journey from Bombay, he led us in a sunrise meditation right in the front of the bus station.

Suddenly, the noisy thoroughfare became a garden of solitude and meditation. In the cool, fragrant darkness I became aware of flowers, palm trees, and tropical vegetation nearby, as well as an inner silence I could not have accessed except for Gurudev's impromptu satsanga.

Time and again amidst difficult conditions, Gurudev would pause near a bus or train station and decide on the spot to hold satsanga—among cows, crying children, beggars, and impatient passengers. If a site appropriate for meditation was not nearby, he would create one.

He reminded us to look beyond the harsh conditions, to see the signs of light and truth that lay behind them. He told us to be like the Hansa, the legendary, divine swan who is able to extract pure milk from a solution of milk and water. Gurudev was always able, as Bapuji would say, "to see the truth through the lie," or as another saying goes, "to see the goodness through the garbage."

— *HARI SHARANA*

your manifesting personality plays a part in your transformative process. You see with less judgement, guilt, or self-reproach.

Your joyous embrace of all aspects and expressions of yourself invariably results in absorption in all the situations of life you encounter. Whatever integration you experience internally always shows up in your daily interactions with life. Through your clear commitment to living in the moment, you express everything you are. Abundant enthusiasm flows into you, more than ever before in your life. On the surface, you may appear to be much as you always were, but internally you are living in a whole different world.

I am living what I am telling you; I work from this plane of consciousness. I am perpetually integrating this awareness into my life. I do not claim a certain state of consciousness, because I live in perpetual openness for the unfolding consciousness. I have no need to judge the level of consciousness at which I am manifesting.

My personality continues to come through everything I do, but I do not try to manipulate it or struggle against it. When I accept my humanity, I come through the trappings of my human personality like Houdini through an impossibly binding trap. The door to ultimate transformation is open to me because I resist nothing, and I want nothing different from what is. There is nothing I try to change, suppress, or withhold about my personality. I am simply in the moment with myself and my experience.

In each moment I am aligning myself with the universal now. This is my ultimate commitment in my life. The whole universe comes and knocks at my door in *now*. Only if I am willing to respond to that knock without any conditions can I open myself to receive reality, the life that is the ultimate gift and the grace of the Guru.

So be completely dedicated to your transformation and live your commitment to be in the moment. Your commitment will then act as a springboard for you to jump off from your familiar past and courageously leap into the unknown future with total trust and faith in life. That trust will give you greater safety than anything your security-seeking mind can ever provide. You will not be affected by anything external, because in the present moment, where you are living, all is complete within itself, including the way you are and the way your life is manifesting.

When you commit to living in the moment, you release being the achiever of your goals, the victim of the past, the dreamer of the future. You enter the perpetually fulfilled moment of now. You open the space for Divine Providence to enter. That divine presence will carry you into a mysterious world beyond the comprehension of your rational mind, in which all possibilities can manifest for you—possibilities completely unattainable through self-effort and struggle.

You need only let go.

The universe then begins to create life for you, effortlessly, because you have gotten out of the way. In that dimension, you do not have to achieve or manifest in accordance with your pre-established concepts. You do not have to control the events of your life or manipulate them to be a certain way. You do not need skill to carry you forward. All you need comes from another dimension—the dimension of grace.

That is called living in the dimension of effortless effort. By being in the moment, you enter into *guru kripa*, the grace of the guru within. Grace comes from trusting the results to come, without knowing what they will be. Such grace is the nectar of existence and it brings resolution to every problem ever created in your life, without your struggling, achieving, or trying to be anybody, anywhere, for anyone.

When you live in openness and receptivity to what presents itself to you, there is nothing you have to do. All existence becomes you, and you become all of existence. ◆

*You need only let go.
The universe then begins
to create life for you, effortlessly,
because you have gotten
out of the way.*

GOD'S WILL

Let the present moment,
no matter what it is,
be your life's joy.

The way you wish
the moment to be
is your will.

Whatever the
present moment gives you
is the will of God.

Align yourself
with the will of God.

Say in this moment:
"Thy will be done, not mine."

God's will is revealed
from moment to moment.

God lives
in the present.

Be in the moment
with God.

"YOU ARE MY SADHANA"
Gurudev's Message To His Disciples

Whenever I think of you, my disciples, my heart pours out love to you. I want you to know that I have given my life to you. I am yours all the way. I have no other purpose in my life but to grow through loving and serving you. There is nothing I have done in many years, and nothing I ever want to do, but love all of you.

I was born in my heart center and loving comes naturally to me. You can rely on the continuity of my love, because it is my nature to love you. To me, you are my beloved children, the very extensions of my soul. You are the sparkling gems of the heart center through which I function and in which I dwell.

You, too, have become worshippers of the heart center. Our worship of love came to us from Bapuji, who lived his life as an incarnation of compassion. Bapuji taught us that love for God and for every living being is our sadhana. He demonstrated that loving God can never be separated from love for every person in your life. Although Bapuji's sadhana appeared to be solitary, through his consciousness he actually extended his vibrations of love to all of humanity, reaching people's hearts on a vast level far surpassing the capacities of normal human contact.

My life's work is to love God by loving every one of you. Bapuji gave me his shakti because he wanted to extend his energy in a direct way through me to you, his grandchildren. That is why this work we are doing together is a manifestation of Bapuji's consciousness. I am deeply grateful that that great master selected me to be his instrument in serving you. You are the fortunate recipients of Bapuji's grace, passed to you through me in our spiritual lineage of love.

A Ride From Darkness to Light

It is dawn, and light enters into the darkness of the new spring day.

This ride to the airport is different from others I have shared with Gurudev. Gurudev is quiet, looking out the window, commenting on the beauty of the morning. The fog hugs the ground in blankets of soft grey. Gurudev talks about the dawn as his favorite time of day. The morning opens into light, and the miles slip beneath us quietly and gently.

I am aware of the quietness of Gurudev's passive grace—the wordless, silent presence that he brings to everything. Somehow, in the company of fewer words, I relate to him more easily. I am with him, simply by being with him—the way he always is with me.

The trip is smooth and uneventful. The quiet peace in our car is broken only by an occasional chant of Gurudev's.

We pull up to the terminal. Double-parking, I jump out, get Gurudev's luggage out of the trunk, and walk over to him. He is stretching, totally awake and alert, already absorbed in the next thing.

As we say our goodbyes, there is a moment's hesitation on my part. I never know when hugging is appropriate with Gurudev, how it fits into my working with him. In the past, I've managed to convince myself that hugs aren't part of my job description.

Today, however, Gurudev looks at me, senses what I need, and opens his arms wide. In the brief moment of his hug it becomes clear to me that love exists as a thing, not different from a thing called gravity. Love is a natural law, a phenomenon of the universe, and Gurudev is channeling it.

As we part I mumble something to him about loving him so much. He smiles his perfectly boyish grin, turns on his heel, and is off toward the check-in counter and the next event.

I lean on the hood of the car for a moment's grounding. I know profoundly in this moment that the love Gurudev offers me has nothing to do with me. It has nothing to do with anything I do or don't do, how well I perform, or the level of my discipleship. Love simply exists in the universe, like gravity, and Gurudev channels it into whoever or whatever is open and available. The woman in the blue hat, getting out of the car in front of us, is fully offered his love. The airline representative checking him in will be offered the same love. It is up to each of them, as it is up to me, to receive it.

Gurudev exists as a channel of universal love. Untouched by bias, preference, or prejudice, he pours back into the universe the love that already exists, the love that flows through him. His love is untouched by conditions, untainted by desires, unfiltered by ego. It is absolutely and totally impersonal. It simply is.

Driving home to the ashram, I sit with myself, in tears, in gratitude, in full knowing; there really is nothing to do, no acceptance to get, no approval to win.

I drive home, freed by Gurudev's universal love.

— ARUNI

By making that perceptual shift in how I see you, I am more able to connect with my own soul in my sadhana and bypass my mind and ego. Loving and accepting you has become a practice of loving and accepting myself.

Your love has touched the deepest part of me as nothing else has. I thank you. Thank you for surrounding me with your love, being with me, and providing me this opportunity to love my soul by serving yours. Our relationship is an exchange between us, in which my ability to receive your love is equally as important as the love I give you. If I could not receive all the love you give to me, if I perceived myself only as the one giving love, I would be exhausted. It would not be a true relationship; it would not obey natural law.

In nature, all beings are involved in an interplay of giving and receiving. The earth nurtures and feeds the tree, giving it strength and beauty. The tree sheds its leaves, which enrich and become part of the earth's soil. If the tree or the earth tried to do all the giving, without receiving, natural law would be broken and growth would end. You and I are like the tree and the earth. Our love supports each other's deepest growth. Our mutual ability to receive each other creates a circle of energy that constantly feeds itself.

You are my sadhana. As I guide you through your obstacles, I see the way through my own. The more I love you in your times of fear and unhappiness, the more I work through my limitations and inhibitions. Though I may have worked through the fears that you are facing, I have other inhibitions that arise at the level of consciousness in which I am functioning. When I help you find your inner light, my clear light comes through me.

Like any human being in relationship, I am tempted at times to react to the story being presented by your ego and mind. However, my reaction to your human story is very brief, and I move quickly beyond it to connect with your soul instead.

I want to reassure you that I love you without any obligation on your part. I expect nothing from you. I don't consider our relationship as one in which I am doing something for you, because everything I offer you is offered on a soul level, and on a soul level there is no difference between us. Any support or care I extend to you comes back to me many times over, without my seeking anything in return. I honestly feel that there is no difference between us and that you are the extension of me.

I have not come to teach you, but to love you. I teach you by the way I love you. How I love you shows you your path for loving one another and everyone you serve. I model for you the path of transformation through selfless service that Bapuji taught me.

My heart center is my human vehicle for divine love, through which I bring you the message of God and guru. Only through my heart can I communicate to you the depth of the divine love that I feel, the divine love that you are. Without

words, love teaches you all you need to learn, for everything you need to know is already within you. My greatest teaching occurs through my being a catalyst for you to awaken to your inner knowing.

I speak directly to your heart, bypassing the mind. You receive me in the subtle space of listening that exists beyond the reaches of your mind. Through our wordless communication, I give you the whisper of divine love. Our nonverbal communication far surpasses anything I can teach you intellectually.

Our relationship is an energetic exchange taking place between us on subtle levels. To expand your capacity to attune to our energetic communication, practice the verbal teachings I have given you and do your sadhana. Your practice of my verbal teachings attunes you to a place of stillness and receptivity within. In that state of stillness, you can receive my love at the frequency I deliver it. That is the way for you to expand your capacity to resonate with me.

Trust

One Christmas, many ashram residents caught terrible cases of flu.

Although I was determined not to succumb, I woke early one morning with achy bones, glassy eyes, and a high fever. I stayed in bed for several hours as my condition worsened. Finally I grew so weak I couldn't get up to go to the bathroom.

I lay in bed, sweating and feverish, feeling as if the slightest movement would be my last. Someone came to bring me tea and tell me that I would soon be moved to the ashram infirmary.

Then I heard a tap on my door and Gurudev entered the room. He was visiting all the sick residents. As he walked to my bed, he stopped suddenly and turned to pick up a stick of incense that was lying on my altar. He handed it to me, saying, "Burn this." Then he put his hand on my forehead, cooling me with his touch. "I hope you feel better soon," he said lovingly as he walked away.

Soon afterward two people came to move me to the infirmary. When they helped me sit up I noticed that my head wasn't pounding and my body wasn't aching. In fact, to my surprise, I realized I was no longer feeling sick at all. I looked in the mirror and saw that my eyes were clear. I decided to go to the infirmary, nonetheless, and I burned the incense for everyone there. Since I had no temperature and felt fine, I left at lunchtime and went back to seva in perfect health.

I realized that my quick cure came from my faith in Gurudev. All he did was give me incense, touch my head, and say a few loving words, yet the degree of trust I had in him made his actions healing and I was healed.

Since then I often think of that day and remember the power of my faith. My experiences with Gurudev have led me to trust completely his intentions for me. Over and over, my trust in him has led me to breakthroughs during the most difficult and challenging times of my life.

— *KARUNA*

*I will always be here for you
in your hour of need.
The connection to guru that
you have built in your good times
will sustain you and give you faith
in times of crisis.*

It is not necessary for you to be fully on my vibrational level before communion takes place. It is enough that you are with me with a sincere intention to grow. Your whole life is a continuing opportunity to come into the vibrational state of love and consciousness that I represent to you. There is no need for you to assess or judge where you are in your consciousness. Your practice is enough.

Only you, my disciples, have the capacity to understand what I am saying because we have bonded at a soul level through our relationship. I have become your soul mate and you have become mine. This soul connection extends throughout our Kripalu family of disciples, for no one understands your search of the soul better than your fellow disciples.

You are always protected, through me, by our lineage—our beloved Dadaji and Bapuji. There is nothing you will face in the course of your discipleship that I will not assist you with, nothing you'll go through that you'll endure alone. I will be ever at your side, supporting you through the soul connection we share.

I will always be here for you in your hour of need. The connection to guru that you have built in your good times will

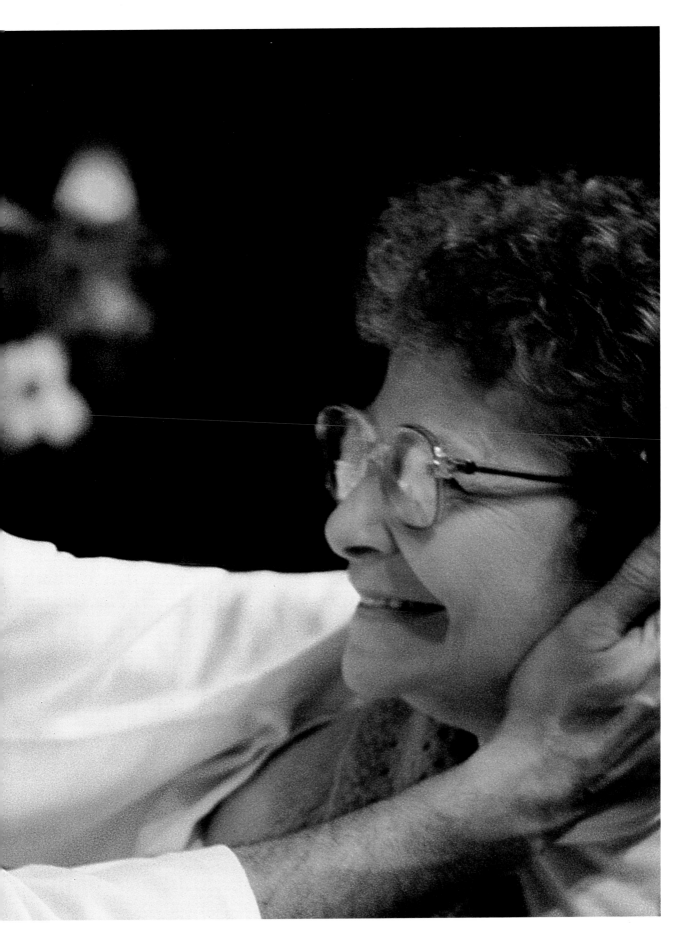

sustain you and give you faith in times of crisis. The faith and love you have developed all along the way will allow you to access the love and protection of the guru. When you are at a crossroads in your life, or when you are confronted with an overwhelming situation, invite me to be with you in spirit. Call on my presence. Make me your best friend. I will be there.

Our relationship is a journey from the external guru to the inner guru. Its ultimate purpose is to lead you beyond your relationship with me to one with your own inner guru. When you walk on the path I have shown you, you walk with the guru who dwells within your being. I am here for you in the early stages of your journey to help you find and follow that higher self.

When the time comes, my final act of love for you will be to help you move beyond the form of our guru-disciple relationship, because our external relationship will have completed its purpose: you will have come home to yourself. That day will bring me personal joy and my greatest fulfillment. ◆

Snapshot

Once Gurudev offered me a snapshot of his inner world.

One of his close disciples, a friend of mine for whom Gurudev has much love, was planning to move out of the ashram. It seemed to many of us that the resident was running from a personal conflict rather than facing it.

Gurudev was describing to me the pain he experiences when he sees us make choices that seem to take us away from our core, our inner guru.

Gurudev's words were soft and calm. "I could," he said, "try to persuade this person to stay." He looked away, his gaze distant. "Yet," he continued, "that would violate natural law. He needs to do whatever he needs to do." He looked back at me. "And I need to allow life to be."

In that moment I saw Gurudev's commitment to release continually any attachment to his disciples, even when such attachment could be seen in a spiritual light.

Gurudev is completely human, with deep personal feelings for us as friends who share his path. But his love for us and his service to us goes beyond the power of a friend's influence. The essence of the guru goes far deeper. Willing to provide guidance when it's requested, equally willing not to interfere once we make a choice, he allows each of us to play out our own karma, the lessons for which we were born.

— *BRAHMANAND*

The Vision

Two years before I met Gurudev I had an experience with him that literally saved my life. I was in an intense depression resulting from my discovery that my wife was seeing another man. My life felt empty and ruined and I wanted to end it.

I was living in Chicago. Without a thought I walked down to Lake Michigan. It was a spring night—beautiful, starry, and clear. There was no moon in the sky and not a person in sight. I shuddered in the chilly night air, unprotected by my denim jacket.

I started walking into the water, with the intention of not coming back to shore. The water was frigid, but I didn't pay attention to it; the wind was icy cold, but it had no impact on me. I walked farther into the water, until I was up to my knees. My life flashed before me: my marriage, my pain, and all the feelings of despair that engulfed me.

I kept wading into the lake, the water first reaching my waist, then up to my chest. I stopped and stood in the water, physically numb, and looked at the stars.

I felt as if time had frozen, that the stars would never move again, that all life was focused on me. Suddenly, a huge face appeared in front of me like a vision in a dream, taking up the whole horizon. It was clearly an Indian man with long hair.

He said to me, "You don't have to do this."

And I said back to him, "Why not?"

He said, "Turn around and go back." I was feeling so much, yet I was numb. I saw the face and I saw the stars, but I wanted to keep going, farther and farther into the water, into oblivion. He said to me once again, "Turn around and go back."

With his final words, something deep inside me shifted. I turned and waded back toward the shore. I felt uplifted and warm inside, my sense of sadness fading.

Life went on. I remained upset for a time, but the intense depression was gone. My marriage dissolved and with the love and help of friends I recovered and continued my life. I forgot about my experience in Lake Michigan.

Two years passed before I actually met Gurudev, and several more before I remembered that night in Lake Michigan. I realized then that it was Gurudev who had come to me in my moment of despair. It was as if he had called me back to fulfill my destiny with him. Even before I met him, my guru had been with me, leading me to safety.

— PRABHAKAR

I have not come
to teach you,
but to love you.
I teach you by
the way I love you.
How I love you
shows you your path
for loving one another
and everyone you serve.
I model for you the
path of transformation
through selfless service.

The Mirror

Because of the clarity of his consciousness, Gurudev has been an excellent mirror for me, reflecting again and again who I am, especially when I'm not seeing myself clearly.

In the summer of 1990 I returned from an eight-month stay in India with a plan to leave the ashram after fifteen years of residency. I had no fully-formed agenda; I just wanted to experience living out in the world for awhile.

I discussed my plans with Gurudev. I told him I really didn't have "reasons" for leaving, that it was a "choiceless" decision.

In Gurudev's teaching a "choiceless choice" is a free response to the happening of the moment, undistorted by attachment based on past conditioning and desires. After many years of residency I had become a pretty smart puppy when it came to using the teachings to justify something I wanted.

Gurudev asked me if one of the reasons I wanted to leave was to explore romantic relationships. I said, "No." He said, "Romantic attraction arises from our sexual energy, which does not always manifest as overt desire. It can subtly motivate our actions without our conscious awareness."

That was the first mirror Gurudev held up before me that day. Only later did I realize that such attractions *were* influencing me, even though I hadn't been facing that fact.

Gurudev teaches that the mirror of my consciousness gets clouded in areas where I am attached. Often he holds up a clearer mirror that shows me what I may not otherwise be willing or able to see.

"Attractions are natural," he said, "but if they are motivating you without your awareness, you are being controlled by them."

I went on to tell Gurudev that I questioned whether there was a place where who I am fit in with the community. I felt I needed to express my particular individuality apart from the ashram, that having to "fit in" was holding me back.

Once again Gurudev revealed me to myself, with a second mirror: "Look at my life," he said, "and the obstacles I've faced. Did I let them stop me from expressing myself? Beyond that, look at the amazing opportunity the ashram provides. It is like a field of consciousness—so many people concentrated in one place, focusing on expressing a greater freedom of consciousness. So much support and love, so many avenues of self-expression. If you can't express yourself fully here, will you magically do it elsewhere?"

"I don't necessarily disagree with what you are saying, Gurudev," I responded. "The bottom line is that I just feel moved to leave. It feels choiceless."

With obvious love, he said "I don't know that your decision is truly choiceless. But I am open to the possibility that your words are true. I respect you and love you. Whatever you do, know that you always have my love and the love of this family. If you choose to go, you have my blessing."

I had moved into the ashram in my late teens and grown into adulthood under Gurudev's fatherly nurturing and guidance. Now he was playing the role of mentor, saying, "You are free to choose and learn from your choices—free to enjoy or suffer from the consequences of your decisions."

He was mirroring to me that I was responsible for my life. I had been all along of course; I was the only one holding me back. I let myself be affected by this final reflection he had compassionately mirrored to me. His nonattached reflection and love triggered in me the ability to see myself with similar nonattachment.

As I dedicated myself to a more objective process of self-discovery, I began to see that I was being motivated unconsciously by desires to do, have, and be something I thought I was held back from at the ashram. The energy I had previously put into departure plans became available for uncovering all the ways I have stopped myself from expressing fully in the here and now.

Once that happened, I realized that I dwell in my consciousness, not an external structure. Taking responsibility for both my growth and my personal expression, I have chosen to continue to live in Gurudev's ashram at this time and direct my energies toward freeing myself from self-imposed, inner limits so I can express who I truly am.

I'm grateful for the clear, loving mirror of Gurudev's consciousness, and grateful for my own commitment to place myself in front of it.

— *SHIVANAND*

DELIGHT IN WAKING UP

Believe in the goodness of your soul.

*Acknowledge how well
it has guided you.*

*And yet, know
you will fall asleep along the way.*

*When you sleep,
take no delight in blaming yourself.*

*Take delight
in waking yourself up once more.*

*Self-blame is the deepest injury,
the deepest sleep of all.*

*Wake yourself up with ultimate
gentle affection.*

The Flute

For a period of time at the Sumneytown ashram, Gurudev was on a wholehearted campaign to get us up in the mornings to do yoga sadhana. He would visit the dormitories in the early morning darkness, playing his wooden flute to wake us.

I remember being pulled gently from sleep by the music of his flute, waking into awareness of myself and Gurudev in the same moment and feeling the sacredness of the new day surrounding me. I would think, "Ahhhh, Gurudev's here," as the melodious sounds of his flute called me to consciousness.

Then Gurudev went into a period of seclusion. Unfortunately, my sadhana practice began to wane. Like so many other disciples, as soon as the master left I lapsed into forgetfulness.

One dark, cool morning, as I slept soundly, there were several loud knocks on my bedroom door.

"Are you up?" Knock, knock, knock.

"Who is it?" I managed.

"It's Gurudev."

"Come in," I said, half-asleep.

And in walked Gurudev, the fiery Shiva, the guru of transformation. He walked straight to my bed and said to me, "Why are you in bed? I've told you to get up!"

I was impressed that Gurudev cared enough to come all the way from his apartment to the brothers' dormitory at half past four in the morning to support me in getting up to do my sadhana. I felt as if I were a sleeping disciple in the Garden of Gethsemane, with Jesus standing before me, asking, "Why are you asleep when I have told you so many times to stay awake?"

As I quickly put on my sadhana clothes, I felt deeply touched by Gurudev's loving care and the consistency of his commitment to us. He was always there, day after day, shaping the community, training the disciples— over and over without fail. Even now, many years later, I sometimes awaken to the memory of Gurudev standing at the foot of my bed, reminding me to wake up.

— *DINABANDHU*

ON THE ROAD WITH GURUDEV

In my role as a director of Kripalu seminar programs, I have often found myself on the road with Gurudev, driving, flying, or riding with him to various locations. I love to see new places and meet new people, but what's more important, traveling with Gurudev has revealed to me where I am "on the road" of my spiritual journey home to God, aided and abetted by my guru.

The Radio Interview

Gurudev has always shown me unconditional love in every situation no matter how klutzy I've been. One time I drove Gurudev to a radio interview in Reading, Pennsylvania in his big Oldsmobile. I was very anxious about driving. We got into the car and I said, "Gurudev, would you like to drive?" He said, "Oh, no, no. You drive." "Really," I said, "it would be fine with me if you drive." He said, "No, you drive."

I am five feet two inches tall, and to me driving a big car feels like steering a yacht. I couldn't quite reach the pedals with my feet. Because of that, I had a hard time accelerating smoothly. When I started the car, we were both thrown back abruptly against our seats as the car lurched and bolted down Gurudev's driveway. Sensing my anxiety, Gurudev said gently, "That's okay. Sometimes things like that happen with automobiles. You pulled out just fine."

After forty-five minutes on the road we were only halfway to Reading and the interview was to begin in ten minutes. What's more, I realized I had forgotten the directions to the radio station. Dying of embarrassment, I confessed, "Gurudev, I don't have the directions." He said, "Oh! You don't have the directions." "No," I repeated robotically. "I don't have the directions."

I watched Gurudev shift into an attitude of acceptance. There was no make-wrong, no annoyance, no "What happened that you didn't bring the directions?" He simply said, "Well, pull over. Let's ask that man over there." We pulled over and Gurudev, in his usual light-hearted, cheery way, got the directions from a stranger.

We were now late and still had another twenty minutes driving time. Gurudev put some lively Indian music on the radio. He took off his sandals, perched cross-legged in his seat, and kind of boogied to the music with the joy I always see in him, no matter what the circumstance.

We *finally* arrived at the radio station. I went to get the Kripalu flyers out of the trunk for the interviewer. Staring numbly into the empty trunk, I realized the flyers were not there—I had forgotten them. It was the third time that day I'd screwed up.

Gurudev could justifiably have become irritated or frustrated, or even given me a gentle reprimand. There was nothing like that. He just said, "We'll make do with what we've got." Gurudev simply would not allow anything to change his intention to give acceptance to me and to be in joy with his experience, whatever that experience was. We did the radio interview, got in the car, and headed back to the ashram.

He spent the whole drive back entertaining me with stories of his Indian boyhood in his hometown of Halol. I asked him, "Gurudev, did you know as a little boy that you were conscious? Did you have a sense of your destiny? How did you get the way you are?" He said, "I got the way I am because whenever there was a chance to give, I gave. And when it was time to let go, I let go. That is how my consciousness has emerged. It is as simple as that."

Gurudev was expressing exactly what I had experienced him demonstrate to me the whole morning. From his standpoint he was never a victim of what was happening because he was always in the position of giving to me, even when my shortcomings seemed to be taking away from him. And he was always willing to let go and live in whatever reality brought him.

Cruise Control

Another time, I drove Gurudev between our two Pennsylvania ashrams, thrilled to be with him. We were going sixty miles an hour and Gurudev said, "Vidya, use the cruise control." I said, "But I don't mind having my foot on the pedal." He said, "No. You should use the cruise control." I said, "But why Gurudev?" He said, "Try it. Just try using the cruise control."

I put on the cruise control, which I had never used before. I settled my leg and foot into just relaxing, which meant I had to trust the car to go at its pre-set speed. He said, "What do you feel?" I said, "I had to let go in order for the car to go into cruise control."

He said, "Do you get it?" I was still a little slow on the uptake. I repeated back, "Uh, do I get it?" He said, "Yes. You know, we do the same thing in life. We think we have to keep our foot on the pedal. The fact is we could go into cruise control and just let grace carry us where we need to be when we need to be there, trusting that we can reassert control if that becomes necessary."

In The Hall Of Stalin

In the fall of 1990 I traveled with Gurudev to Moscow where he had been invited to introduce the Soviet-American dialogue on yoga to a crowd of hundreds of people. We were gathered in a mammoth hall that had not been open to the public since the days of Stalin. Through Gorbachev's reforms, the public buildings were now open for people to use.

For decades, yoga, like other spiritual practices, had been suppressed in the Soviet Union. Now here we were, come together publicly in the name of yoga. Most of the participants were Soviets, but there were people from all over the world, cutting across all social and professional lines. Gurudev was the keynote speaker, entrusted to guide the opening of the entire conference.

In off-white shirt, slacks, and shoes, our tall, elegant guru strode onto the enormous stage. The curtains drawn shut behind him were golden, so he was a vibrant cream color against a golden background. A Soviet interpreter came out to translate Gurudev into Russian, a very pleasing language to listen to.

Gurudev began to speak, guiding the hall of hundreds of people into meditation. I sat with my eyes closed, thinking, "I cannot believe this. I am sitting in meditation with my guru in the Soviet Union, in a huge international gathering with one common purpose: experiencing peace."

My heart was taken by the feeling of predestination in the experience; it was as though we were all together fulfilling some higher plan from a blueprint drawn up long ago. I opened my eyes and looked at Gurudev. To me, with his dark hair and closed eyes, he was the Prince of Peace, sitting in meditation in a state of utter balance and tranquility, the personification of unconditional love. Following his meditation, the hall was profoundly silent.

Then Gurudev began chanting a Shiva mantra. I felt something occurring in that pregnant space among us all that was totally beyond what our logical, linear minds could create through understanding or rationalizing. It was as though in that moment Gurudev mobilized and personified our collective souls' dreams of peace and oneness on this planet. We were lifted to a place of tremendous possibility.

Within minutes, we were all together—Soviets, Germans, Americans, French, Dutch—chanting a resounding chorus of "Om" that echoed through every brick, wall, and pillar in that newly reopened hall of Stalin's. I thought, "The peace we pray for on this planet is occurring right here in this room. This moment is as powerful a peace pact as has ever been spoken by any world leaders. It is as powerful as the dismantling of any nuclear warheads."

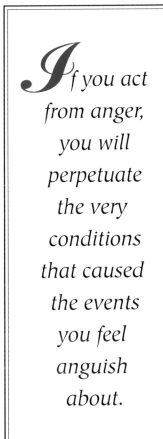

If you act from anger, you will perpetuate the very conditions that caused the events you feel anguish about.

Midnight Train To Leningrad

After that amazing experience, Gurudev and I took the "Midnight Train to Leningrad." It sounds like a Forties movie and the experience for me was just as intense as one.

When most of us visualize having close, personal encounters with Gurudev, we envision a scene of tremendous devotion, wisdom, and bliss. Actually, working closely with Gurudev usually presents an opportunity for him to expose our egos and humanness to us in ways no one else possibly could. He is so insightful and so sharp in his ability to see through acts and masks that when he senses a willingness and receptivity in us to look deeply into ourselves, he can be a true Shiva, the power and impact of his words laying bare our entire personalities. Something like that happened on our trip to Leningrad.

I was considering leaving the ashram and expanding my own teaching into Europe and I had been going through a tremendous amount of pain and internal struggle over the issue. I was trying to see where my calling fit in with my community commitments and my discipleship. I asked Gurudev if I could discuss the subject with him during our train ride. We sat in the soft lights of the midnight train, as the lights of Russian homes sparkled past us from the darkness outside our window.

First Gurudev offered me an apple, again offering to me, always offering. We sat nibbling and chatting. He said he wanted to risk telling me the truth about my ego. He pointed out dark holes in my ego that I hated hearing about.

For example, he pointed out how often I insist on seeing things my way instead of broadening my view to see them through the eyes of others. He went tenderly and gently, and yet he went truthfully. He can be ruthless in telling the truth as he sees it, but he is always gentle. He's always ready to hand me a Kleenex or an apple and say, "It's going to be okay. And here is the truth." At that moment, more than any other, he held up a mirror for me to look frankly at myself.

When we arrived in Leningrad we flagged down a taxi. I was still recuperating from our talk, my ego having been splattered in a thousand pieces by Gurudev's loving straightness. We got in the back seat of the taxi and I brought up some of what Gurudev had pointed out about my attitudes.

There I was in the back seat of the taxi, crying and crying. The Russian taxi driver looked back at us. He probably didn't know what to make of this long-haired Indian man and Western woman, both speaking another language, and me hysterical. Finally he turned around and handed me some Russian-style Kleenex, which was just some coarse tissue paper, and smiled kindly at us both. I will never know what he made of the whole thing.

We arrived at the hotel and I walked Gurudev up to his room. He opened his travel bag and there was a demonstration of Gurudev's incredible respect for resources. He had some apples he had been given and some little bits of jam and jelly in containers, all of which he had carefully saved. He never threw out anything that had been on his airport or cafeteria trays.

He said, "Here. Sit down, Vidya." He handed me another apple. It was as though he were saying, "I invited your ego to break up and see itself, and now I will help you heal yourself and come back to wholeness." That is the kind of dance Gurudev does with his disciples, the dance of Shiva. Now he was again the gift-giver in my life, reassuring me through little acts of love. Through his combination of straightness and nurturance, I was able to integrate his teachings to me and experience a renewed sense of wholeness and release.

Later in the day we were picked up by our Leningrad sponsor, a very socially oriented psychotherapist, a dedicated humanitarian who had been working in Armenia since the earthquake there. He took us to the apartment of one of his friends for a meal with some of the intelligentsia of Leningrad, a group of people interested in world events and committed to making a difference. There sat Gurudev and seven of us in an upper room, just as we hear about in stories of Jesus. A woman translated the Soviets' questions about social injustice, as well as Gurudev's answers.

64

Gurudev delivered a remarkable body of teachings, the likes of which I had never heard from him—teachings drawn forth by the unique circumstances. Here he was with people who had watched their families and comrades suffer at the hands of the KGB, in concentration camps, in earthquakes, in poverty. Their bottom-line question was, "What do we do with the angst we feel, and the sense of despair and anger that is our heritage?"

The message Gurudev gave them was, "If you act from anger, you will perpetuate the very conditions that caused the events you feel anguish about. You will continue to feed the heritage of fear that created these intolerable circumstances." He invited them to consider making change occur around them and within them, not from retribution, but from *contribution*.

I raised the question to Gurudev about Jesus and his angry behavior with the moneychangers in the temple. It appeared that Jesus felt justified in his anger. I and some of the others told Gurudev, "Even in the life of Jesus, there was retribution or at least reaction." Laughing, Gurudev said, "Isn't it funny how selectively we choose incidents from the lives of saints to justify our humanness?"

Gurudev taught us to look at the whole of Jesus' life, not one event, and recognize that his contribution was one of service and transformation founded on unconditional love. Love was Jesus' theme. His glory came from initiating change through love.

At the end of our Russian trip, Gurudev and I both acknowledged that it was perfect that I had accompanied him, for several reasons. One was my interest in issues of world peace. Another, and more important, was the opportunity to receive the profound learnings Gurudev offered me during that great journey.

On The Road With Myself

Later, after much soul-searching, I did decide to leave Kripalu ashram after fifteen years of residency and continue the worldwide teaching I had begun. The decision brought up for me a question and concern about how my bond to Gurudev would change by my doing work in the world, rather than in the ashram.

In August 1991, Gurudev was about to leave for Japan and China and I was soon to leave for my new home in the Netherlands. Wanting to say "I love you" and wanting the reassurance of his love, I went to see him unannounced, with an enormous bouquet of flowers.

I knew I wasn't following etiquette by going to Gurudev's home unannounced, but love carried me there. I rang the bell and stood waiting with a beating heart. I told myself that he might not be thrilled to see me on his doorstep. I might be interrupting him. I thought to myself, "Don't expect glory. You don't know what is going to happen."

Gurudev appeared at the door, surprised to see me. "Gurudev," I said, "I brought you this bouquet of flowers. I am here to say I love you, and goodbye." He reached out and hugged me and said, "I'm delighted you came to see me. As for these flowers, you are the flower. But your bouquet is beautiful, too. I will keep it on my altar."

He said, "I'll be right back. Wait here." He took the bouquet and went into his house. I heard him moving about inside. I heard little drawers opening and closing. He finally came out with something in each hand.

"Okay," he said, "open your hands." Here once again was my guru, loving me, wanting to give to me, ready to support me. I turned my palms up and he laid in one a pink quartz crystal in the shape of a heart. He said, "This is my heart and it is going with you. Don't worry. My love will be with you." He then placed a clear crystal in my other hand and said, "And this crystal is to give you the blessing that you continue to use your gifts, and be used by them. Lastly, and this is most important, Vidya, I want you to fly. I want you to fly like a bird, free. Let go of all history and just fly." That was his blessing.

My years on the road with Gurudev had prepared me well to embark on the next leg of my life journey, accompanied by the guru within. Two decades of his unfailing acceptance, unconditional love, fearlessness in telling me the truth about myself, and steady, brilliant modeling of consciousness had given me all I needed to step out on my own. I flew both literally and figuratively to the Netherlands and my new home, with Gurudev planted firmly in my heart. In spirit, I am still on the road with Gurudev.

— *VIDYA*

I got the way I am
because whenever
there was a chance to give,
I gave.
And when it was time to let go,
I let go.

That is how my
consciousness has emerged.
It is as simple as that.

GOD IN DISGUISE

To me, every person I interact with is God, coming to me and teaching me how to be. He comes in many different forms. Every person I encounter is God in disguise; he is hiding within each person. When I remove the filters of my mind, God is right there in front of me.

Turkeys

It seems I have a reputation as a good driver, so I am often asked to drive Gurudev to the airport. I love doing it. I feel honored, as if I am protecting Gurudev though my driving skill, like the warrior Satyajit who protects the wheel of Arjuna's chariot in the *Mahabharata*.

One Thanksgiving Day we were driving to Kennedy Airport. It was wonderful being in the car with Gurudev. His energy seemed to permeate the car with consciousness. He sang Ram and Krishna chants as he enjoyed the fall scenery along the way.

As we drove, my ego became involved in the experience. I decided to ask Gurudev a question, and I had an ulterior motive. I wanted him to give me a discourse on something—on anything—my own special darshan. Then I could go home and say "This is what Gurudev taught me" and everyone would know how special I was.

As we traveled down the Cross-Bronx Expressway, I noticed all the high-rise apartment buildings and I thought of the people having Thanksgiving dinner inside. A perfect topic, I thought, to stimulate his teaching.

I said to him, "Gurudev, there are millions of people celebrating Thanksgiving Day with a special dinner right now. What do you think of Thanksgiving?"

He looked up, glancing at the apartment buildings that lined the highway. With a twinkle in his eye he said, "I think it's a bad day for turkeys."

That was it, the extent of his spiritual message. He did not feed my ego at all.

A bad day for turkeys!

— *SATYAJIT*

72

Naturally Himself

Once, years ago in Sumneytown, the trees around Gurudev's house needed trimming. Since I was in charge of maintenance, I called professional tree trimmers to come and do the job. When the crew arrived and piled out of their old truck, I was startled. They were four big and burly macho guys, complete with tattoos and torn jeans. They looked very different from me and the other ashram residents.

"How ya doin', guys?" I asked a bit awkwardly.

As I began explaining the job, I felt uncomfortable. I saw myself trying to conform to their personalities, so I could fit in and relate to them. I felt I had to change subtly, to try to be more like them, in order to talk to them.

I looked up and saw Gurudev walking toward us. He was shoeless and wearing his robe, and his long hair was blowing slightly in the wind.

"Good morning," Gurudev said to the crew. He was friendly and relaxed. As he told them simply and clearly what he wanted from the job, I watched the interaction carefully. The tree-trimming crew appeared comfortable with him, won over by his naturalness. The crew and Gurudev laughed together as they walked away toward one of the target trees.

I was amazed at how comfortable Gurudev was with them. He acted no differently from the way he did with me privately or with hundreds of people at satsanga. I realized then that I had never seen Gurudev alter his personality to be with people. He always seems completely and naturally himself. His realness disarms people, allowing their realness to surface.

I use that experience as a model. When I interact with people who I feel are different from me either ethnically, socially, or personally, I remember that there is no need to adjust who I am. I have learned through Gurudev's example that all I ever have to be is myself.

— CHARUVADAN

73

The Bikers

It was a hot, steamy New York night as Gurudev and I pulled up to the red light. "I'm tired and I want to go home," I thought, dreading the one-hundred-sixty-mile trip that lay ahead of us now that we'd finished our ashram business in Manhattan. Gurudev sat next to me, quietly humming a Ram chant.

The roar of motorcycles interrupted my thoughts as several large Harley-Davidsons pulled up on both sides of our car. Their riders were clad in leather covered with studs, colorful painted symbols, and chains. I cautiously locked my door and began rolling up my window, thinking, "Uh-oh. This city is unsafe. I hope nothing happens with these wild-looking guys, with Guruji in the car."

Gurudev was looking with great interest at the bikers. To my disbelief, he rolled down his window to get a better look. He said to me, "Look at that man," nodding toward the biker nearest him. "He really loves his motorcycle." Then Gurudev waved to the biker, who gunned his engine and waved back, bringing a smile to Gurudev's face. The light changed, the bikers were off in a cloud of exhaust fumes and noise, and I carefully eased our car into the intersection.

"I'm out here on the lookout for fearful situations but Gurudev's out here looking for love," I thought, "and he finds it time after time. Love comes to him because that is what he sees everywhere." I looked in astonishment at Gurudev, who had settled comfortably into his seat for the trip home.

— *GITA*

Gurudev And Bapuji: An Introduction

The early morning brilliance of September in the Berkshires illuminated Gurudev's house as I waited for him in his darshan room. The exuberant singing of Mintu, Mataji's cockatiel, resounded from the kitchen. Gurudev's many beautiful crystals reflected rainbows throughout the room.

Gurudev entered with a warm smile and sat on the floor before me, all enthusiasm and creative energy, ready to work on the manuscript for this book. He had returned just the day before from giving seminars in Japan and China, yet showed no sign of jet lag or weariness. I asked about his trip and we exchanged some pleasantries. Then I introduced the article I had brought for his review that day, an article that had no direct relationship to Bapuji.

But in introducing the article, I made a small, offhand mention of Bapuji. Immediately Gurudev's face softened; his eyes were focused outside on the mountains in the distance and he became silent for a moment. The article was forgotten. Thoughts of his beloved guru occupied his attention.

Spontaneously Gurudev began to share deeply, personally, about his relationship with Bapuji.

Midway through his sharing he recalled a private journal he had kept in India in 1969. During that time Bapuji instructed Gurudev in the secrets of yoga and awakened his shakti. It was one of the most significant times in Gurudev's life. His personal instruction by his master, Kripalvanandji, led him to communicate the ancient, experiential truths of yoga to the West.

Gurudev went upstairs to his office and rummaged around, returning with a green marbled composition book, faded with age. As he read I was moved by the precious, timeless quality of what was taking place. I was filled with love as Gurudev shared his great devotion to Bapuji, and my eyes brimmed with tears when he described Bapuji's love for him. The gratitude and reverence Gurudev described feeling for Bapuji reflected my feelings toward Gurudev; I realized I was learning from my guru what it means to be a disciple. I felt a completion of a cycle of teachings and love passed down through the generations of our lineage of masters.

Gurudev read of a moment when Bapuji, moved with love for his young disciple, could not lift his eyes from his slate to look directly at Gurudev. As he recalled that intimate moment Gurudev's voice broke. Unable to read further, he closed his eyes and wept, immersed in the unparalleled love his guru had showered on him.

What follows is Gurudev's expression of gratitude and love for Bapuji, a moving and personal account of intimate times with his master. Then in his journal entry Gurudev shares with us the poignant moment when he received from Bapuji the secret teachings that became the foundation of his life.

— *EDITOR*

GURUDEV REMEMBERS BAPUJI

*I*t was Bapuji who awakened my heart center. The potential for that awakening was born in me, but the presence of my guru drew it forth from my consciousness. When I met him, my spiritual journey in this life began.

I was only sixteen when I met Bapuji. He was truly *Kripalu*—"the compassionate one"—to me, always extremely loving and kind. He inspired me completely by his way of living. His absolute, one-pointed, uncompromising dedication to God far surpassed anything I had ever seen in any spiritual master. The values by which Bapuji lived and the unwavering commitment he demonstrated to his sadhana revealed the inner vision of God that directed his life.

During the thirty-three years I was intimately connected with Bapuji, I never saw him compromise his sadhana practice. He created his schedule so there would be no distractions and he followed that schedule strictly. His one-pointedness sprang from his love for God.

Bapuji wanted nothing in his life but the highest. His powerful dedication to God was absolutely distinct and unique from what is usually defined as dedication. Every day of his life, Bapuji used each hour and moment for his personal quest for spiritual realization. He meditated ten hours a day, every day of his last thirty years. Whatever time he was not meditating, Bapuji spent writing, to extend the message of his direct realizations to all humanity.

The perpetual pull toward God that directed his entire life never diminished in its intensity. In his commitment to his sadhana he was able to give himself totally, once and for all.

Never did he deviate from that dedication. His extraordinary efforts to achieve self-realization were beyond human capacity.

Bapuji literally lived the saying, *janata janardana*—"every human being is God." His love for others was impregnated with his love for God. Seeing God in everyone, he gave every human being the same love he gave God. In every interaction with every disciple, Bapuji was unfailingly soft and gentle. The love that Bapuji expressed for others was far beyond what we ordinarily call love. To Bapuji, loving humanity was the same as loving God.

In 1977 Bapuji came to Kripalu Ashram in America to visit his spiritual grandchildren. He came for three months; he stayed for four and a quarter years. While he was here, he once wrote on his slate to Mataji and me, "I was born in a loving atmosphere. I was raised in a loving atmosphere. That is why there is one great defect in me. I cannot survive in an atmosphere where there is not love."

While Bapuji was with us, he always felt loved. If he had felt even a subtle negative energy around him or a vibration of disharmony or conflict, he would have left immediately. We felt profoundly blessed by the opportunity to serve Bapuji in his final years as he completed his sadhana living in our midst.

I had the privilege of sitting at Bapuji's feet while he gave numerous lectures and group darshans in our two Pennsylvania ashrams in the late seventies. At each darshan, hundreds of people came up to Bapuji, two at a time, to offer their

pranams. One day, watching these loving "grandchildren," as he called his Western disciples, approaching him on their knees for his blessings, Bapuji gazed at their radiant faces and their eyes shining with love. He picked up his slate and wrote to me, "Do you see God in their eyes?" Bapuji experienced God coming to him through his devotees. Responding to the vibrations of the group at another large darshan, Bapuji wrote on his slate to me, "We have all been together before. These are the old souls who have come back to us. We are connected."

Once when I was sitting with him Bapuji picked up a flower a devotee had offered him and turned it this way and that, marvelling at its perfection. With an expression of wonder on his face he said to me, "Look what God has done."

Bapuji regarded all living things, including plants and flowers, as expressions of divine energy. He worshipped nature with great reverence as a real, direct representation of God. One time I was driving him from Summit Station to Sumneytown. On the way I pointed out a scenic river and said, "Bapuji, look at the beautiful river." He turned in his seat in the car and pranamed to the river. To him the river was a sacred expression of God. That moment was so sweet to me.

Bapuji had very few items in his personal possession: some scriptures, paper and pens for his writing, his slate, and a few articles of clothing. He related to the seemingly inanimate objects around him as expressions of God. He showed great care and respect for each item and kept everything very orderly and clean. He used everything with great awareness and never wasted anything. He did not treat things that way as a formality, but because in his heart he truly felt everything was an expression of the one divine energy that is God.

To Bapuji a pen was not just a pen, it was "sister pen." His watch was "brother watch," and so on. He was in relationship with everything around him, and would regale us in darshan with funny, insightful stories about "sister pen," "brother watch," and other everyday objects the way someone might tell stories about amusing relatives. He treated every object with love. When I was with him, I felt his reverence and love for all things flowing from the source energy within him.

On Bapuji's final day in America before he returned to India, I went to Muktidham to pick him up for the drive to the airport. It was a poignant moment in the ashram: our beloved Bapuji was leaving us, and we knew we would probably not see him again in his human form in this lifetime. With graceful, quiet dignity, Bapuji walked out of Muktidham, the meditation cabin that had been his home and place of sadhana for the last four and a quarter years. I watched my guru as he left that sacred place for the last time in his human life.

Bapuji turned to face Muktidham and slowly, deliberately, put his hands together at his heart in a farewell pranam to the building. Then he lay down on the ground in a *dandav pranam.** He pressed his face into the earth and stretched his arms over his head in a gesture of deepest reverence and gratitude to his place of sadhana. To Bapuji, Muktidham was not a building, it was a representation of the same divine energies that had guided his entire life. He said goodbye to his American home with the same love and feeling with which we would say our final farewell to a beloved friend.

Bapuji's life was his teaching to me, the living lesson that awakened my consciousness. The impact on me of Bapuji's life has far surpassed any verbal teachings ever given by a teacher to his disciple. Bapuji showed me the way to love God through loving humanity, nature, and all existence. ◆

* *a prostration before a being or object of devotion*

82

Devotion

In 1974, I traveled to India with Gurudev and fifty disciples to visit Bapuji and join in the celebration of his birthday. To see Gurudev in the presence of Bapuji was a rare privilege that taught me more about the guru-disciple relationship than I could learn from any book.

As soon as he entered Bapuji's presence, Gurudev changed from guru to disciple. He bowed to Bapuji, then sat as close to his master as he could get without being right in his lap. Sometimes, with tender devotion, he would fan Bapuji; always, he hung on Bapuji's every word with absolute attention.

To speak to us, Bapuji broke the silence that he routinely kept as part of his spiritual practice. He shared with us from his heart, and I was astounded by the self-revealing honesty with which he spoke. He told us humbly that in moments of introspection he could still see faults and shortcomings in himself, even after many years of purification. Clearly, he was not like the gurus who present themselves as flawless and emotionally invulnerable.

Gurudev responded to Bapuji's vulnerability by baring his soul to his master, freely acknowledging his own fears and shortcomings. Bapuji admonished us all to be aware of the ego-intoxication that sometimes accompanies early experiences of the power generated by sadhana.

Though Bapuji was speaking generally, Gurudev used his words as an opening to share humbly with Bapuji about the areas where he, Gurudev, needed to grow. As Gurudev translated for us, he told us that he was taking Bapuji's words personally and using them to make changes in his life. Bapuji said again and again that Gurudev's greatest strength was his ability to admit his faults and errors and to then make whatever changes in his life were called for to prevent the error from recurring.

Gurudev was extremely generous with that which he held most dear: the opportunity to be in the presence of Bapuji. Although he could easily have asked for darshans alone with his guru, Gurudev instead shared the privilege with those in our group and anyone else who made a sincere request to be included. Showering us liberally with his inherited spiritual wealth, Gurudev practiced what he taught about giving to others that which you wish to receive yourself.

In the years that followed, Gurudev would serve his master externally more effectively than anyone could have dreamed, by spreading Bapuji's teachings to every continent on the planet. Yet when I think of Gurudev's dedication to his guru, I will always remember the attitude of pure, unbounded, personal devotion to Bapuji that I had the privilege to witness firsthand.

— *HARI SHARANA*

Shaktipat

Shaktipat is an energetic, spiritual transference in which a master awakens the disciple's latent spiritual energy known as *kundalini shakti* or *shakti*. This energy awakening produces profound, dramatic, and often highly expressive spiritual experiences, frequently accompanied by spontaneous movements, visions, powerful feelings of love and expansiveness, or a sense of releasing long held blocks or fears. The external experiences triggered by shaktipat are an outer manifestation of the inner spiritual awakening occurring in the seeker. The experience of shakti often transforms the inner life of the disciple, inaugurating a new spiritual life and direction. For example, shaktipat can initiate the practice of kundalini yoga, the branch of yoga that involves surrender to divine energy.

The awakened shakti energy acts as a spontaneous purifying agent, clearing the seeker's subtle energy pathways, removing physical, mental, and emotional blocks, and speeding up the natural evolutionary spiritual processes. These processes can be cathartic, much as a physical fast brings repressed physical symptoms to the surface to ultimately improve health, or as a psychologically therapeutic process releases blocked emotional memories from the past to ultimately expand the individual's capacity for greater joy and well-being. As blocks are removed, the inborn divinity of the seeker begins to shine forth.

In *shaktipat diksha*, which is very rarely given, a yoga master such as Bapuji psychically transfers to his close disciple the ability to awaken others' shakti through a glance, a touch, or simply his presence. It is that *diksha*, or initiation, that Bapuji transmitted to Gurudev in January 1971.

Bapuji's intention in giving *shaktipat diksha* to Gurudev was to deliver his spiritual blessing to American seekers through Gurudev. His blessings and direct teachings have now been delivered to thousands throughout the Western world through the teaching and presence of his disciple, Amrit. In Gurudev's words, "What I am is what I have received from Bapuji."

Following Bapuji's transference of *shaktipat diksha* in 1971, many of Gurudev's yoga students and disciples experienced dramatic spontaneous awakenings of their kundalini shakti in his presence. From that time until the mid-seventies, many had intense experiences of awakened shakti in Gurudev's satsangas and seminars simply by meditating or chanting in his presence. And for many, profound experiences of great love, inner joy, and a deep sense of peace followed those sessions.

In the mid-seventies, Gurudev decided to allow only rarely the full expression of shaktipat in his satsangas and sessions with students. He found that the awakening of shakti, while a spiritually moving experience, brought up such intense physical and emotional purification that it could hinder his young disciples' optimal growth in the early phases of their spiritual practice.

Gurudev saw that most people were not ready to receive shaktipat and use it effectively for their personal transformation. He found that the full experience of shakti was too intense for most Western seekers, who still needed to balance their external expressions in practical life with their spiritual awakening. So Gurudev created a more gradual spiritual approach of purifying the mind, body, and emotions through the practice of Kripalu Yoga in balance with a healthy, yogic lifestyle. Through Kripalu Yoga, disciples access in a balanced way the spiritual energies that are awakened

Purity

In the early years of the ashram, Gurudev gave a tremendous amount of shaktipat. Gurus give shaktipat; that's what they do. That was the concept, and there was nothing wrong with it. But the greatest masters became defined as the ones who could give the strongest shakti. Our western minds do that naturally—more is better; if it's good to be rich, then the richest person is the best.

Gurudev would give shakti with the best of them. The rest of us thought the disciple making the loudest noise during satsanga was the one having the highest experience. People knew what a great guru Gurudev was because of the racket his devotees made.

At a certain point, without any announcement, explanation, or justification, Gurudev just stopped giving shaktipat. Deep inside his being, through his clarity, he saw that although his devotees craved dramatic spiritual experiences and the "high" they produce, shaktipat wasn't doing any practical good for the disciples who were not ready for it. Shaktipat gave spiritual experiences. Gurudev's disciples could spend their lives chasing spiritual rushes. But Gurudev knew that a spiritual experience is only a spiritual experience. It is not spirituality. He was committed to teaching the daily practice of spirituality, through sadhana, selfless service, and the miracle of love.

Gurus are human, and they, too, have the tiny filter that might ask the question: "Would people still come to an ashram without shaktipat?" In Gurudev's case, as soon as he realized that shakti would seek its own level naturally, and didn't need him to do anything, he dropped it. He didn't have to say, "Look. I'm really the most spiritual one around, because I'm the one *not* giving shakti." He had no need to say that. He just dropped it. Now *that's* true purity.

— MICKEY SINGER

through receiving shakti and maintain the harmony between their mental, emotional, and physical purification and their path of selfless service.

In developing the practice of Kripalu Yoga, Gurudev formed a bridge between willfully practiced yoga disciplines and kundalini yoga, the complete surrender to awakened energy. In the final stages of Kripalu Yoga practice, the practitioner moves effortlessly into a meditation-in-motion experience in which he or she learns how to surrender the mind gradually to the inner workings of awakened spiritual energy, as a prelude to the full awakening of kundalini shakti. That forms the solid foundation from which the seeker can progress to deeper levels of kundalini yoga sadhana if he or she so chooses.

— EDITOR

"GURUJI IS WITH ME FOREVER"
Gurudev's 1969 Journal Entry

June 19, 1969
Kripalu Ashram, Malav, India

*T*oday is the most gratifying day of my life. Today, in my morning visit with my most beloved Guruji [Bapuji], I spent some immortal moments that have been imprinted so deep in my heart that they cannot be erased by time or space. From this day and time, I feel Guruji is with me forever.

This morning, Guruji asked me to read an article on self-realization through shaktipat. He gave me the explanation of the deepest, hidden truths behind the subject of shaktipat. As his teaching developed, Guruji taught me the depths of the relationship between guru and *shishya* [disciple]. He gave me the example of Swami Vivekananda and his relationship to his guru, Shri Ramakrishna Paramahansa, and Shri Ramakrishna's relationship to his guru, Shri Totapuriji.

Guruji drew my attention next to his devotion toward his *sannyas diksha* guru, Swami Shri Shantanandji Maharaj, at the time of his initiation into sannyas.* He also spoke of his relationship with his *yoga diksha* guru, Dadaji, who gave him initiation into the secret teachings of yoga, including a special pranayama technique that would awaken Bapuji's kundalini.

Slowly, in the process of teaching me about shaktipat and the relationship between guru and disciple, Guruji related the

Following his one and a quarter years of training with Dadaji at the age of nineteen, Bapuji received his sannyas vows from Swami Shantanandji, his second guru. Both the exact date and a precise description of the swami who would formally initiate him had been accurately predicted by Dadaji years before. The story of Bapuji's meeting and training with Dadaji is detailed in Light From Guru to Disciple, *by Swami Shri Rajarshi Muni.*

subject to my relationship with him. Referring to our first meeting, he said, "You were a young boy of sixteen when you met me. You loved me. You got the chance to see my yogic kriyas and serve me at that time.

"You went to America. All this time you have been there, you have never forgotten me. You have always brought your guru to the forefront. You have always loved me. In spite of many adverse conditions you have had to contend with, your love for me has never wavered.

"So soon in your life, you are so centered and set on your goal of yoga. Your experience is so much like that of the many great souls of the past. This I call the grace of God. This same grace is the divine guidance behind me now, giving you these deep and hidden teachings of yoga.

"You are my first disciple. I am teaching you what I have not taught anyone in the past and may not teach again in the future.* I want you to teach all my close disciples. Normally, I do not like to speak of these things, but when I teach you, I am very much inspired. Sometimes I even forget the time and break my schedule of sadhana.

"I am giving you what I have not given to anyone so far. I want you to keep these teachings completely secret, even from your dearest friend. You will understand their true meaning and value when you tread the path of yoga. These teachings will truly fulfill the purpose of your sadhana.

"I pray that God may bring you this truth soon."

As Guruji spoke, his eyes were only on his slate. Normally when he writes for me, he looks up at me occasionally with very loving and expressive eyes. But today, as he wrote on his slate, my most beloved Guruji did not raise his head.

With his eyes on his slate, Guruji just went on writing. I could clearly feel that Guruji's heart was filled with love and compassion. During this time, he was almost in tears. He was giving me such deep secrets of yoga, and blessing me that I might easily come closer to the spiritual goal. His deep feelings in these moments were evident to me.

I know that Guruji has given me the greatest secrets of yoga, secrets that cannot be read from any books. They have been given to me to be nurtured, practiced, and delivered to the rest of the world. ◆

---

* Later, Bapuji also gave special teachings to six other close disciples: Shri Rajarshi Muni, Shri Vinit Muni, Shri Yogeshvar Muni, Shri Asutosh Muni, Ma Om Shanti, and Shri Shubha Darshan.

You have never forgotten me.
You have always brought
your guru to the forefront.
You have always loved me.
In spite of many adverse conditions
you have had to contend with,
your love for me has never wavered."

Bapuji to Gurudev
June 19, 1969

In November 1970, Bapuji sent Gurudev the following letter, inviting him to India to receive shaktipat diksha *from him.*

My son, Amrit,
Jai bhagwan.

In my letter from Eral* I asked you to come here for my birthday celebration and plan to stay with me in the ashram for five days. I am now writing you the reason for that invitation.

In ancient times, the *Brahmavidya,*** which is known as the *yoga vidya*, was given only to the rare and most deserving disciple: one who was not attached to worldly temptations, one who desired only *moksha* [liberation], and one who possessed divine qualities. Only he was considered to be a worthy disciple. Through his grace, the guru used to give such a worthy disciple *shaktipat diksha*. After receiving this *shaktipat diksha*, the disciple would start yoga sadhana automatically and nothing had to be taught. The practice of sadhana would lead him to the highest spiritual consciousness.

There are about five yogis in India that I know of who can give this *shaktipat diksha*. In foreign countries also, there are one or two Indian yogis who give *yoga diksha*, or *shaktipat diksha*. When I heard about them, I felt it must be God's will. That is why I thought to prepare you to give this *shaktipat diksha* to your students so that your worthy mission will become very easy.

Give this *shaktipat diksha* to only two to four disciples who are not attached to worldly desires and who are of good character and conduct, so that your work will remain alive and progress.

When you were here last time [June through September 1969] for higher training with me, I gave you only light shaktipat to help with your future progress. If I had given you powerful shaktipat, you would often have been disturbed in your present activities, and you would suddenly have left all your worldly work to go deeper into sadhana. But I did not give you that powerful shaktipat, because it was my desire that you go into full sadhana only after you had organized your activities there.

This time, I will seat you in front of me and will bestow upon you the yogic power to give the *shaktipat diksha* to others, so that this tradition remains continuous. Remember that shaktipat does not fail even on one who cannot enter into yoga sadhana with enthusiasm and peace of mind, but such a sadhak cannot reach the highest stages.

The rest I will discuss with you in person.
Your loving Bapuji

Gurudev responded with reverence and gratitude to Bapuji's invitation and returned to India. He received shaktipat diksha *on January 7, 1971. Bapuji confirmed the momentous gift that he had bestowed upon his disciple with this message:*

Now, when you return from India after having *shaktipat diksha* from me, you will be able to bring many great changes in the atmosphere of America. Whatever progress you have made in bringing the message of yoga so far was only ordinary. Now you will be able to give these higher teachings as a true representative of God. Your message will become more powerful and popular, and will be of great service to mankind.

On January 12, 1971, as Gurudev was about to leave for America, Bapuji gave him another message. It was read aloud before all the disciples at the Malav Ashram:

You have started your real yoga sadhana abroad in America, so that land has become your land of *tapascharya*. Now I pray to God that one day you will return to Bharat [India], after becoming a yogi of the highest order, so that I may be proud of you.

My God is not imaginary. He appears to me like you all appear to me. It matters little, then, if I call that God the truth, Brahman, Shiva, Guru, or Radha Purushottama. He is everything to me. I feel that he is more real to me than this whole world. May his grace descend upon you all, ever protect you, and attract you toward him.

With blessings, your beloved Father,
Kripalu

---

* A small state ruled by a maharaja with whom Bapuji was staying.
** The secret wisdom of Brahman, or God

*"I received shaktipat diksha from my beloved Guruji,
January 7, 1971, at eight-thirty a.m."*

Entry from Gurudev's journal, Malav, India, 1971

One day I put my hand affectionately on Amrit's head and asked him if he would grant a request of mine. He agreed readily. I advised him to postpone his marriage for five years. He went home and talked to his parents about that. The next day his good parents came to me and said, "Swamiji, Amrit is not our son, but yours. We will have him married when you wish it."

I was touched and pleased by their humility and by their implicit faith in me. They respected my wishes and Amrit married late. That accounts for the fact that thirty-eight-year-old Amrit looks like a youth of only twenty-five. My Gurudev with his good wishes for my welfare had advised me to practice purity of mind, purity of food, and celibacy. These same principles I give as my heritage to my sons who want to follow me. Amrit, being one of the few, has inherited those three principles.

— *Bapuji speaking about Gurudev to Gurudev's*
yoga students visiting Malav, India in 1969

Darshan With Bapuji

In 1980, when Bapuji was living in Muktidham, the small, secluded meditation house in the Sumneytown ashram, he gave Gurudev a private darshan twice a day.

The darshans were an enormous privilege for Gurudev, a gift to him from his beloved teacher. Bapuji's strict dedication to a secluded life of meditation was well-known; he observed silence most of the time and did not allow any distractions to his sadhana. Yet he invited Gurudev to be in his presence twice every day for special teachings. Being with Bapuji was the single most important thing for Gurudev.

One day Gurudev was meeting with a group of residents engaged in a lengthy discussion about ashram policy. The time approached for Gurudev's afternoon darshan with Bapuji.

"Gurudev," someone said, "it's time for your darshan."

Gurudev responded, "Being with you is my darshan with Bapuji."

His words brought tears to my eyes. I was touched deeply by Gurudev's willingness to sacrifice time with his master in order to serve us and by his devotion to the essence of spirituality rather than its form. For him, doing the work of Bapuji was equivalent to having Bapuji's darshan. That's the way Gurudev always interpreted his relationship to the guru. Gurudev stayed with us until late in the afternoon—until the issues at hand were resolved.

Since then, when I'm offered an opportunity to serve that conflicts with my personal plans, I remember Gurudev's teaching. If he could sacrifice being with Bapuji to be with us, then I can sacrifice my preferences when called upon to love and serve another.

— *CHIDANAND*

"Beloved Amrit"

I will now tell you a little about beloved Amrit. He has been closely associated with me since he was only sixteen years old. We both feel natural affection for one another. If someone were to ask me, "Among your householder disciples, whom do you consider best?," I would definitely nominate beloved Amrit first! I would not suggest Amrit only because I love him like a son, but because he is genuinely deserving. Truly, this deservedness has not come to him all of a sudden, however; it has developed gradually. Who does not make mistakes? Everyone makes mistakes, so beloved Amrit must have also made various mistakes. But since he is a vigilant sadhak, he is interested in finding his faults, and he remains aware so that they are not repeated.

Amrit is extremely loving; he is fond of sadhana, the saints, and the scriptures; he is ambitious and restrained, and he is extremely in love with me. Once no one had ever heard of me here in America; but he placed my portrait faithfully in the ashram meditation room, and to this day he has worshiped it as if it were a god. He has also invoked love for me in the hearts of thousands of disciples. Is this not devotion to his guru?

For the past two and one-half years I have lived very close to him and have had a chance to observe directly the complete scope of his life. Really! He is a high-caliber householder sadhak who lives the life of a saint. One day, with his throat choked with emotion, Amritji came to me and said: "Bapuji, kindly let us know if there are any remaining shortcomings in our service; do not hesitate in the least. Without feeling at all embarrassed, we will immediately improve upon the shortcomings."

Such affectionate utterances can only slip out of the mouth of a close disciple. Amrit and Urmila, and their entire spiritual family of disciples, have served me with total love and dedication. I am greatly satisfied with this. I convey my heartfelt blessings to each of them.

— *from Bapuji's 1980 birthday discourse in America*

Love's Expression

All my life I had heard people talk about love. In movies, books, songs on the radio—everywhere—the word was tossed around casually. By the time I got to the ashram I was more than a little confused about what exactly love might be. It wasn't until I had the opportunity to observe Gurudev closely in the role of disciple that I began to understand.

In the last photo session I had with Bapuji before he returned to India, I spent several hours photographing Gurudev and Bapuji together. It was only months before Bapuji passed on, and he was physically weak.

Gurudev's concern for Bapuji's comfort was a tangible force in the room. Every change in Bapuji's position was accompanied by Gurudev's rearranging Bapuji's cushions, robe, or shawl. Any possible need of Bapuji's was anticipated well in advance by Gurudev. Every idea I had for a different photo angle was presented carefully to Bapuji by Gurudev to make sure it was acceptable to him and would not cause too much strain or discomfort.

Bapuji did not ask for that attention. But the depth of love that Gurudev was feeling for his guru called out for expression, and Gurudev responded with exquisite tenderness, precision, and care.

Bapuji commented several times on the extraordinary quality of love in "Amrit's" service to him. Watching Gurudev's face in the moments when he received Bapuji's praise told me everything about the heart of a true disciple. I saw neither pride nor self-satisfaction in Gurudev as he received Bapuji's appreciation; rather, there was great humility, reflecting the inner fulfillment that came from serving the one to whom he owed his spiritual life.

By observing Gurudev's love and service to Bapuji, I received my first glimpse of the quality of love that I, as a disciple, might offer to my guru.

— *PANDAVI*

ENERGY AND CONSCIOUSNESS

Everything we see around us—indeed, everything in existence—is a play of energy and consciousness. Energy is the basis for each form of life that exists on this earth and consciousness is the life behind each living being. In every stage of creation, the hand of consciousness is present. Consciousness is the enlivening force of all living beings existing in the universe.

God is the Cosmic Soul, the source of Unity Consciousness or Oneness. The spark of God is divided among innumerable, individual embodied souls. Every being in the cosmos is an embodied expression of God's spirit. The impulse of life originates in God and expresses itself through the individual life form it takes.

The cosmos you see is made up of millions of representations of the one Universal Consciousness embodied in different forms. Each stone, tree, plant, and mineral has its own consciousness. Every place you look, in everything you see, consciousness is present.

The spiritual journey of life, which evolves through many forms, is a return to the original, undivided Oneness. Our evolutionary journey is motivated by a deep, inborn drive to realize our inherent Oneness. Whatever a living being experiences, and whatever stages of life that being passes through, the end result is the return to God, Unity Consciousness, Oneness.

All forms of life known to us reach their evolutionary climax in human life. The human being represents the highest level of embodied spirit, where consciousness has come to its greatest refinement and expression. In no other form of life is consciousness found as focused and individualized as in humankind. We human beings are conscious of our existence in a way that is unique and different from any other life form in creation as we know it.

The natural world around us is always in transition, change, and evolution. When we observe the lives of animals, trees, plants, rivers, and all the other life forms teeming around us, it becomes abundantly clear that everything in the cosmos is in constant unfoldment. The difference between us and the other forms of life is that only humans have the ability to resist or react to the evolutionary process.

Wouldn't it be funny if autumn came and the trees were all in mourning over

Therefore, everything you experience is a perfect expression of the play of consciousness focusing in your being. Whatever you feel, and whatever you have felt since you were born, is playing an absolutely necessary part in your transformation and unfoldment. If you feel fearful, it is necessary to your evolution. When you feel angry, it is necessary to your transformation.

There is nothing you can experience that is out of the cosmic order of your unfolding consciousness. There is nothing that surfaces from within you that you need fear or resist. It is all a play of the evolving consciousness that you are, expressing through you and transforming you.

Wouldn't it be funny if autumn came and the trees were all in mourning over their leaves drying up and falling? Nature continuously conveys the message to us to accept reality as it is manifesting.

their leaves drying up and falling? Nature continuously conveys the message to us to accept reality as it is manifesting.

As the cosmos is in constant evolution, so is the human being. When we suffer or go through difficulties, we, as conscious embodied spirit, are simply expressing our natures to grow and change. From that perspective, all that we feel and experience is part of the evolutionary impulse, manifesting through the various expressions of our lives. The evolutionary impulse focuses through us and helps us evolve.

Due to our unique faculty of self-awareness, we humans have the ability to be mindful of our experiences and use our lives for our evolution. By remembering that we are consciousness, manifesting as embodied spirit, we can realize that whatever comes to us has a place in our evolutionary journey. Thus, we have the opportunity to use for our highest good the diversity of events, struggles, and challenging situations that make up our lives.

We each have a choice whether to participate in our evolutionary process by

learning to encounter our fears and difficulties consciously, or to resist and struggle
against our experience. Through our
choices and our awareness, we can either
accelerate or slow down our growth and
evolution.

When we react negatively to the play
of consciousness manifesting in our lives,
our minds engage in "foul play" by inter-
vening in our experience and resisting
what is happening. Resisting our natural
evolution is as unnecessary as the autumn
tree fighting the loss of its leaves and the

departure of summer.

We have the capacity to stop the growth-
inhibiting power-plays of the mind and
thereby actively support our evolutionary
process. Through spiritual practices that
teach us to encounter life consciously, we
can prevent the foul play of the mind from
blocking our evolution.

Practicing Kripalu Yoga and meditation
increases our awareness and, with it, our
ability to be witness to the ups and downs
of life. The practice of yoga enables us to
enjoy without fear or resistance the play of

energy and consciousness expressing within us and around us.

As you move through the stages of human life, remember that you are spirit, the interplay of energy and consciousness. Then you will play your many roles with great joy and love in your heart, knowing you are the spirit behind their manifestation.

By remembering that you are on an evolutionary journey, you'll embrace what life brings you with peaceful acceptance, and allow it to transform you. You will trust that as it does in the entire cosmos, the energy of consciousness is working perfectly within you at all times, for your highest evolutionary good. ◆

Whatever you feel, and whatever you have felt since you were born, is playing an absolutely necessary part in your transformation and unfoldment.

Communion

In 1985, I traveled with Gurudev to St. Croix to assist him in the first seminar he led there. Before that time, I had seen him only in formal, structured settings, and traveling with Gurudev opened for me a whole new way of perceiving him as I witnessed his spontaneous experience of nature.

Gurudev in nature is magnificent. I watched him as he opened every pore of his being to take in the natural beauty that is St. Croix. He was totally himself, without agenda and unconfined by any formal role. I watched him move through the days as if he were a primal, natural animal guided only by pure instinct and prana.

One moment in particular is engraved in my memory: Gurudev standing on a white sand beach, framed by the turquoise ocean and clear sky, the sun on his shoulders, his hair blowing around his face.

Time seemed to stand still. There was no other place in the whole universe for him to be in that moment—nothing to do except to be wholly with himself. He allowed nature to move him. It was as though St. Croix were breathing him.

I watched Gurudev jump into the ocean. He did not approach the water with the attitude, "Now let me take a swim." He jumped in as if he *were* the ocean, wave returning to wave. When he came out, he didn't reach for his towel; he became the sun and the air. Where he lay was irrelevant to him. He did not lie on a blanket, but on the fine, white sand.

Gurudev dissolved into the environment and the atmosphere. His totality with everything drew me into communion—with him, with nature, and with myself. Witnessing Gurudev's spontaneous freedom, I learned how to enter into absorption and experience another level of possibility for my own being.

— *BRAHMANAND*

The Tenth Day

In 1971 my mother was taking yoga classes with Gurudev in Philadelphia. She considered him a friend and spiritual teacher, and always trusted the purity of his heart. Gurudev had told her that no matter what happened, he would always be there for her and for her family.

Gurudev had just returned from India where he had received *shaktipat diksha* initiation from Bapuji, enabling him to transfer shakti, or energy, to others.

When I returned home from college for semester break, I took a yoga class with Gurudev to learn more about this man that my mother was so impressed with. I didn't know anything about gurus or spiritual paths, but when I met Gurudev I immediately felt connected to him.

Before I could attend another yoga class, I came down with a severe cold and developed serious infections in both ears. I was very ill and had to visit a medical clinic daily to have my ears lanced and drained. The ear specialist kept increasing my medication since the infections wouldn't heal. I was on my third prescription with no results. I sweated so much from fever that my mother had to change the sheets on my bed five or six times each night.

Days passed and, as the infection raged in my ears, my mother grew more and more concerned. On the night of the tenth day, as I prepared for sleep, desperately uncomfortable with both fever and pain, my mother said, "Enough of this! I'm going to call Amrit and ask him to pray for you. I don't know what else to do." As I lay in bed listening to her walk away, I had a feeling deep inside that something important was about to occur.

After a few minutes, my mother came back into the room, and as she adjusted the blankets over me she said, "Amrit is going to pray for you tonight." She tucked me in, kissed my sweaty forehead, and walked out of the room.

I did not sleep one moment that night. All night long, I was a tossing, turning, burning ball of energy. The fever broke. By morning the fever was gone, leaving me exhausted, yet somehow renewed and energized.

In the afternoon, my mother and I returned to the ear specialist. He looked into my ears with his instrument, paused, and looked again. He shook his head in disbelief and said, "Both your eardrums are completely healed. There is no inflammation." He looked over at my mother and asked, "What's happened here? Is this some sort of miracle?" My mother and I just looked at each other in shared, silent wonderment.

That event completely hooked me and my entire family on the magic that is Gurudev. I went to every yoga class he offered. Soon after, when Gurudev opened the Sumneytown ashram, I moved in to study and learn from him. Today, after twenty years of living in the ashram with Gurudev, I continue to be blessed by his love.

Gurudev never said a word about whether or how he had played a role in my healing. From others I have heard similar stories of physical and spiritual healing involving Gurudev, but he has never encouraged such stories and has always maintained an attitude of quiet humility about such matters.

— *JYOTI*

"You Missed Your Chance!"

One night at Shadowbrook, the chapel was filled with visitors and residents. Gurudev was calling on people in the audience who had questions for him. He called on a guest, who stood up in the very center of the room.

"Yes?" Gurudev asked. "What is your question?"

The man looked at Gurudev for a long moment, then blurted out, "Can you perform a miracle?"

My heart stopped. I felt the whole room hold its breath in hushed anticipation. "This is it," I thought. "This will really be great." I felt frozen in place with expectation.

Gurudev, without missing a beat, asked the man, "What would you like to see?"

The guest hesitated and seemed deep in thought for a moment. He said, "Well, I'm not sure."

Gurudev replied, "You missed your chance!"

After a long pause, the entire room broke into laughter, with Gurudev's merriment leading the way.

Gurudev went on to teach about the miracle of love. Again he showed me that though my mind longs for supernatural proof of spirituality, those external experiences are not where miracles lie. True miracles exist in the depth and beauty of the teachings of the masters.

— CHIDANAND

*Everything you experience
is a perfect expression
of the play of consciousness
focusing in your being.*

MEDITATION: RELAX INTO BEING

When you sit in complete silence and meditate, you bathe in the energy that is constantly bubbling through you, all around you, and throughout all of existence. You participate in the celebration of life. You do not have to create this experience; it is there waiting for you all the time. You need only be silent and acknowledge it.

When you are a silent participant in meditation, your silence is an invitation for the divine energy to make itself felt. Your meditation is an emptying process: the letting go of your desire to achieve something. You stop struggling to control your experience or shape it into what you think you want. The moment the emptying happens, you become intimate with the energies that are all around you, all the time. You become the recipient of the grace that is born within you and always surrounds you.

Unfortunately, we are seldom silent. Our inner silence is constantly interrupted by our struggle to achieve our idealized concept of meditation. Our self-created expectations of having a certain meditation experience prevent the true experience of meditation from taking place. The more we struggle to achieve a particular experience, the more that struggle disturbs our inner silence.

While our minds are busily designing our ideal meditation and struggling and efforting to achieve that experience, we are completely missing the divine energy that silently surrounds us. Our planning, achievement-oriented mental processes obstruct our internal silence by trying to make something occur that is already present within us. In other words, we get in our own way.

In our worldly existence, we have become accustomed to using effort and struggle to develop ourselves and to solve problems. We try to use the same tools when we meditate. We try to force a pre-conceived inner experience that we hope will solve our problems. But when we apply our worldly methods of trying and achieving, we are unable to discover the solution to our real problem.

Our real problem is resistance to the experience of *now*, this present moment. In the name of achieving some ideal in our minds, we deny the reality of our experience in the present moment.

Every solution we arrive at is a disguised denial of the now.

By trying, we are searching for the solution to a problem we only think we have. That solution, even if found, will never satisfy us, because it addresses an imaginary problem of our mind's creation.

Meditation is not a future-oriented process of getting better. Meditation is the experience of now. It is a process of embracing who you are, fully, in the moment you are sitting in meditation.

If you attempt to make your meditation better out of dissatisfaction with your experience, you create tension between what

114

Surrender to Ecstasy

The following is my attempt to capture my experience witnessing Gurudev's Kripalu Yoga posture flow:

I was at the Florida seminar in 1991. The man who'd been talking to us from his chair in the front of the gymnasium walked to an open space in the center of the room. Among the hundreds of observers, he kneeled casually. I was crammed among several others—not uncomfortable, yet not free to unfold my knees in a full lotus posture. Nothing in Gurudev's presentation had prepared me for what I was about to experience.

Gurudev's body began to move. The others present receded from my awareness. The room could have been my own study or a childhood meadow: some private, secret place unknown to the world at large. Solitude folded her vast petals to embrace the two of us: movement and stasis, creator and observer.

And I began to *see* clearly. The smudged windowpane through which I'd been viewing my life instantaneously became dazzlingly lucid, washed clean by the energy of life itself that was subtly surging through the moving limbs of this yogi. Through this crisply focused lens that my eyes had oh so naturally shifted into, I saw a figure whose movements were the tangible truth I'd always wanted to know: a dance of plainspoken eloquence.

The shapes his body assumed in the yoga flow were not speaking any language I'd ever memorized, yet somehow I was hearing his silent movements with my remembering eyes. The rattle of life ceased with the emergence of this bold form drenched in light—not the light of a spotlight shining down from a high-towered heavenly kingdom, but the solar radiance of a human heart burning its purity through the hidden hurts within me, reaching to the very center itself, my unblemished soul. He offered me my own divinity through his humble exposé of our mutual innocence.

In a split-second of the greatest autonomy I'd ever known, I chose to recognize reality, and in that deliciously risky moment, the universe unhatched with a quiet roar and only he—light, joy, freedom—and I were in it, after all. No oppressors existed in this revelation of the harmony that has always been. His movements bespoke *everything*, withholding nothing of himself—so far beyond cynicism, bitterness, and all dank, unpleasant things that he was weaponless as a child.

Free! Indomitably alive! I am this! Yet, paradoxically, in that moment his body, rather than mind, was articulating my own heart's overflow. No loss. No loss. His unshieldedness invited me to risk annihilation simply because no danger exists. For such is love.

The elixir I'd longed for in every pursuit and relationship of my life was here; this individual's existence contained for me the guideposts to Beauty's origin. My struggling ended here in an old gymnasium in a crowd of strangers as I looked upon this true person who had suddenly revealed himself to be the living textbook of answers: so shatteringly personal in his impersonal expression.

— *ULKA*

*Meditation is not
a future-oriented process
of getting better.
Meditation is the
experience of now.
It is a process of
embracing who you are,
fully, in the moment.*

is and what you think *should be*. Your effort to deny or change what *is* generates mental turmoil, which makes you feel anxious, tense, and impatient. You then may begin to judge yourself for not having a good meditation. Those mental gymnastics block your ability to be still and, without inner stillness, you cannot access your inner source. Through struggling to get better, you have actually gotten in your own way.

Again, in worldly affairs, effort is praised and considered effective, but in meditation, effort is a liability. If you *try* to be totally present, you will miss the energetic experience I am describing. Your attention will be focused on trying hard, which is the opposite of what I am talking about.

Your mind is constantly trying to create experiences and ignoring the energetic experience waiting inside you. To have that experience, no effort is needed. Simply be, and acknowledge what exists within you. You cannot achieve a meditative experience; you can only discover it.

Meditation is a turning within, a return to the source of the light that is reflected to you by your external experiences. Looking outside for solutions to your life situations is like looking at the reflected light of the moon and believing it to be the sun. When you realize that the moon's light is only a reflection of the sun, you don't sit in the moonlight when you want to get warm. Similarly, if you want to enter into your own light, you don't misplace your attention onto changing your external experiences.

To meditate, and enter into the source within, you must create silence within. Then you can acknowledge the flow that is constantly nurturing you, sustaining you, and feeding you. For example,

117

when you chant "Om," the energy and vibrations caress you and love you. They hug you. But are you really there?

To receive that divine caress, let yourself be conscious and relaxed, in a state of not expecting and not wanting. To bathe in the energy, be as present and relaxed as possible. Do not force your experience. There is nothing to create. You are simply returning to that which is your true nature. By being inwardly silent and physically tranquil, you'll return to the natural balance and repose that is your true self.

Meditation is total acceptance of what you're experiencing right now. As you accept your experience, you develop receptivity to what is being revealed to you in each moment through your body, mind, and emotions.

There is no moment without your willingness to experience it fully. Being totally present in your experience and welcoming each moment, whether you are pleased or repulsed by it, creates an opening for reality to come to you. Your true nature can be accessed only through total acceptance of the present moment's experience.

Trying is achieving. Being is discovering. Meditation is an attitude of waiting and discovering. You are waiting to discover something that already exists and is immediately available to you. You can only discover something that exists and is waiting to be seen. When you can wait to discover the moment, exactly as it is revealing itself, you do not have to make an effort to achieve a particular experience.

Take an inner pose of silence, waiting, and discovering. The less you do, the more you will be. In the moment of silence, true meditation shows up, right here, to bring you into the ecstatic experience of now. When you are not there, God is. ◆

Trying is achieving. Being is discovering.
Meditation is an attitude of waiting and discovering.
You are waiting to discover something
that already exists and is immediately available to you.

119

Nice, Even Spacing

By some strange quirk of fate, in my early days as a resident I was given the role of ashram photographer. In those days, staffing decisions seemed based on divine whim rather than practical skill level. The person least prepared for a job sometimes seemed to get it. That was certainly true in my case.

I was a star-struck twenty-year-old in the honeymoon phase of my discipleship, and photographing Gurudev ranked for me in the realm of celestial occurrences. The possibility that I, a mere mortal, would be working closely with him caused several simultaneous reactions in me, ranging from unabashed joy to panic and the inability to swallow.

At our first meeting, I presented myself to Gurudev, stiff and solemn as a soldier on a mission. Every time he asked a question or gave an instruction, I would respond as though I were undergoing interrogation at the hands of the enemy. I wrote wild notes, scribbling his exact words, accumulating dozens of garbled follow-ups that raced in some unidentifiable language up and down and across many pages.

Gurudev observed me patiently. Then he asked to see what I had written. After a quick review, he smiled and said, "Here, let me show you how to take notes." He calmly demonstrated how to make straight lines and columns on a sheet of paper. "Like this," he offered, handing it back to me. "Nice, even spacing so you can read it later."

My brain went on "hold" as he looked into my eyes. In the midst of my acute embarrassment, there were those eyes, reflecting acceptance and humor, inviting me into the moment.

What is it like to be loved by Gurudev? He uses the utter simplicity of each moment to live in and love from, and shows me a world filled with the potential of consciousness. "Nice, even spacing so you can read it later" has become a touchstone for my devotion to the ordinary and my reverence for what is. I have learned from Gurudev that consciousness and love are not mythic events taking place on some grand, cosmic scale, but real experiences happening right now within the mundane details of my life.

Gurudev has an innate artistic connection with life that keeps him continually in the realm of consciousness and creation. A constant stream of fulfillment and joy flows from him, as well as a refusal to believe in limitations or critical barriers. I, on the other hand, used to inhabit a world of strict, tight boundaries. What was possible and what was impossible were clearly distinct, and questioning the distinction, to me, bordered on heresy.

On one occasion we were planning the filming of "The Path of Love," the movie that depicts the life of Bapuji. Gurudev wanted to create an Indian-style celebratory procession, with Bapuji in a gaily-decorated pony cart, followed by disciples in colorful saris and festive clothing. It was to be a striking visual scene, and I was assigned to organize it. I was taking a lot of notes.

I was feeling panicky, and pressing Gurudev to make a decision about the sequence of events. "It'll never work, Gurudev, unless you decide exactly how things will go." As he looked at me his eyebrows furrowed, signaling his disagreement with my conclusion. He peered at me and said, "Pandavi, don't try so hard to do exactly what I say. Don't follow me mechanically. You have to respond to what's happening in the moment. Not just in photography, but in your whole life. Respond to what is." I had rarely seen Gurudev so emphatic—I think he could see that I was using rigidity as an ineffective technique to feel secure and in control.

As I watch Gurudev over the years, his ability to respond spontaneously in every situation astounds me again and again. He never goes on automatic—whether he is taking a walk, driving his car, or sitting in a business meeting. His joy in spontaneous creation is always tangible and infectious, and makes being with him irresistible. In Gurudev's presence I feel I too can let go of any artificial limitations or security systems and joyfully embrace my own spontaneous creativity.

— *PANDAVI*

PERFECTION

Recognize that
you cannot be
any other way
than the way
you are
in this moment.

Recognize that
you cannot be
in any other place
than the place
you are
right now.

Become one with reality.

Align yourself
to the truth
of what is.

Discontinue association
with the past.

Drop dreams
of the future.

Live in the perfection
of what is.

Attunement

For three years before I met Gurudev, I had an active case of Crohn's disease, an inflammation of the ileum. Medical science has no cure for the disease, and even with potent medication the best that can be hoped for is temporary remission. I had begun taking cortisone soon after the condition was diagnosed.

When I met Gurudev, I immediately felt drawn to him and started listening daily to tapes of his chanting. As I listened, I let go of thoughts and entered into physical experience. I allowed my body to sense the chanting vibrations. I started to feel better.

Over time, my symptoms of Crohn's disease decreased significantly. I called my doctor in New York and told him I wanted to stop taking cortisone. He was horrified. "You can't do that," he said. Nevertheless, after a few more symptom-free months, I stopped taking the medication.

Instead of it, I stepped up my practice of Gurudev's teachings. For six months, I spent seven hours a day doing sadhana, organizing my practice around my job and my responsibilities to my husband and two children. I spent another six months listening to Gurudev's lecture tapes for hours at a time, transcribing them to share with other devotees in my Kripalu support group. I practiced Gurudev's presence constantly, asking myself, "How would Gurudev be in this situation? What would Gurudev think or say?" When I saw Gurudev, I would find myself sitting the way he sat or walking the way he walked. I absorbed Gurudev as much as I could.

After ten symptom-free years, I returned to the doctor for an examination and x-rays. He studied my x-rays with amazement. "I have never seen anything like this," he said. "You had a serious case of Crohn's disease. If someone looked at these x-rays today, he would never know what condition I treated you for. In my experience, I have never known anyone to go off medication and have their intestines heal. I have no idea how this happened."

I, however, *do* know how it happened: by my attunement to Gurudev through chanting, being in his presence, and practicing his teachings. With Gurudev's help, I have changed whole thought patterns and how I relate to stress. I have changed who I am, and that is what healed my body.

— *SHANTIPRIYA*

CONSCIOUS RELATIONSHIPS

*Y*ou express yourself and experience life through your relationships. Therefore, relationships play an important part in the journey of your soul. How you relate to the people in your life forms an integral part of your growth and transformation and either enhances or restricts your spiritual evolution.

Spiritual growth is merely a philosophical concept if you separate it from your friendships, family, and working relationships. The fact is that you develop consciousness through your daily interactions with others. By learning to be conscious with a loved one, you learn to be conscious in all areas of life. The spiritual lessons and experiences that result from your relationships ripple out to transform the way you work, play, and be with yourself.

To approach your relationships as part of your spiritual journey requires an in-depth understanding and application of the principles of spiritual growth. You must understand that your soul yearns to return to its original oneness with God, and that in your journey home to that state, the false concepts, dreams, and suppressed feelings and fears that block your ability to be fully conscious come to the surface to be resolved and released. Everything you experience in your life is part of that surfacing process.

All the evolutionary processes a soul goes through in its journey back to God are found in the microcosm of human relationship. As human beings, we live together and form close bonds with each other as expressions of our inner yearning to complete our evolution and return to oneness. Our

125

relationships with each other vitally support us as we learn to release assumed images and suppressed feelings.

Through the dissolution of our expectations of our partner and the past fears we have held about relationship, we integrate ourselves with reality. Our search for union in our relationships thus serves as a perfect vehicle to return us to the greater union for which, on a deeper level, our soul is searching. Our conscious use of the difficulties in relationship gives momentum to our evolutionary process, our spiritual journey home to God. The ecstasy of that spiritual reintegration far surpasses the temporal happiness we dream about achieving in some ideal relationship.

You are revealed to yourself every time you interact with another human being. In encountering one person, you can see the way you treat all human beings, including yourself. How you think about other people, judge them, and hold expectations of them—and how you react when they don't meet your expectations—all send clear signals about yourself. All your reactions show where you are stuck or fearful or holding on and what you need to heal within yourself.

Treat each person as if God has come to teach you through that person. As you learn to be fully present and accepting of each person you meet, you transform yourself. You learn to embrace and love the whole universe through that one person.

In marriage, the opportunity exists to use relationship with another person either for spiritual growth or for failed expectations. A spiritual seeker has a foundation for marriage that is totally different from that of an average person.

In Western culture there is no strong

foundation on which to build a marriage, since marriage here is based on the fantasy that another person will fulfill our dreams of being happy and loved. Along with that fantasy comes the anticipation that another will design his behavior and lifestyle to be totally complementary to ours.

With that falsely-founded fantasy in place, the possibility for a long-lasting marriage is doomed from the start. When our expectations are not fulfilled, we

You are revealed to yourself every time you interact with another human being. In encountering one person, you can see the way you treat all human beings, including yourself.

become angry, frustrated, and hurt. We feel betrayed. Somehow we thought that the other person existed simply to fulfill our expectations, which grew out of a feeling of incompleteness that we made up in the first place. Our inability to understand and work with unfulfilled expectations is the cause of the high divorce rate in the West.

When we fantasize about what our lives will be like with our partners, our experience of them is dominated by our expectations, through which we evaluate each of their behaviors, attitudes, and actions. The *real* relationship then becomes unacceptable to us. Our anticipation of what our partner should be like and how he should make us feel creates an enormous conflict with reality that prevents us from evolving or growing spiritually or even enjoying our lives in the simplest ways.

In the spiritual model, our relationships are our sadhana, providing lessons to learn about ourselves and opportunities to grow during our journey back to God. If a relationship is not spiritually based, it cannot work. It will become a constant source of aggravation, disappointment,

and pain. In a spiritually based relationship, we take the position that we are not in the relationship to change our partners, but to use the relationship as an opportunity to change ourselves.

Paradoxically, once you take conscious ownership of your relationship experience, you receive the fulfillment with your partner that those with the wrong foundation strive for and miss. By letting go of wanting the outer relationship to assume a particular form, and working instead only on transforming yourself, you begin to bring to the relationship such expanded consciousness and loving acceptance that both you and your partner are tranformed.

Your internal changes may be reflected by a deep change of attitude and expression in your beloved. But keep your eyes always on your own transformation. By letting go of demands that your partner behave a certain way, you bring greater joy and peace of mind to yourself and open the door for him to transform positively as well. Never let yourself forget that your partner's change is not necessary for your growth and well-being, nor is it what you are looking for.

Our personal history can block our ability to use relationships for growth. We bring to every relationship the history of all the relationships we have had and all the undigested, unfinished experiences from them that we still carry subconsciously. We are rarely present with those in front of us. Sitting between us and them is the cloud of our unfinished relationships, filtering everything they do and say and coloring our experience of them.

In addition to our generic historical filter, in any intimate relationship we are also holding onto our specific history with that person. Every suppressed feeling, undigested experience, and thwarted expectation looms over our interactions like a storm cloud waiting to burst. When conflict arises, our stored-up past rushes in like a thundershower and distorts our perception, drowning out the interaction in a flood of pent-up past grievances.

We find it difficult to solve the problems that arise in relationship because we cannot see reality. Our lingering history and our dreams of future happiness turn into expectations of our partner. Those expectations, in turn, prevent us from seeing our partner, and our relationship with him, as both exist *right now*. Our expectations act as one more filter that keeps us from dealing with exactly what is taking place in front of us.

It is not easy to overcome your past history and future dreams of relationship. To do so requires a lifelong practice of becoming conscious. There are, however, certain steps you can take in daily interactions that help you drop the filters of unfinished karma in your relationships. With every movement in that direction, you experience greater fulfillment and satisfaction, even though you still have more to do to complete the process of emptying the unconscious.

To make your relationships more conscious, use whatever comes up to work on yourself, and only on yourself. Transformation and change in relationship come from taking full responsibility for your fears, projections, and unclarity. To do that, you must be willing to face your fears about your partner and your relationship.

Instead of working on ourselves, we usually try to control our partner's behavior, which is less risky and uncomfortable than facing our fears. When we face our

Reflection

Gurudev teaches that we create our own reality. The way we love ourselves and others becomes the way others love us. An experience I had with Gurudev moved this teaching from my mind to my heart.

Gurudev and I were at a seminar given in a college, and we were walking down a stairwell in the college's main building. I know from experience that Gurudev acknowledges every person he passes with a loving, joyous glance. On this occasion, because I was walking behind him, I was able to look over his shoulder and observe the reaction of each person as he or she encountered Gurudev.

No matter what expression people approached with, an incredible glow came over their faces as they came closer to Gurudev. Whether or not they had met him before, their eyes brightened. I could feel their hearts opening and their love pouring out to Gurudev. Each person who passed was obviously affected by his energy.

As Gurudev loved those people unconditionally, he received love back. No matter what feelings people were initially experiencing, it was love they ended up reflecting back to him.

I apply what I learned that day on the stairs in my own life as I move toward creating whole relationships. The way I love other people is the way they love me. If I choose to withhold my love, to be greedy or angry, then that is what returns to me. But if, like Gurudev, I extend love, then that is what I receive. It's my choice.

— *RAJIV*

fears, we may feel out of control and want even more to focus our attention on changing our partner. The truth is that we *are* completely out of control of our partner. We must exercise control where it belongs: on ourselves!

When you let go of your need to control your partner, real solutions begin to emerge. You begin to see into yourself and release the fears from the past and fantasies of the future that hold you back. Every time a conflict arises in a communication, you choose to reflect on your own thoughts and actions. You begin to see how you create your experience. You also see how your suppressed past and expectations of the future support your false interpretation of your partner's behavior.

The biggest obstacle to focusing only on yourself in a conflict is the desire to blame your partner for the way you are feeling. The moment you blame, you renounce self-observation and lose all possibility of finding the true solution within yourself. In blaming, you desert the territory of your inner landscape where resolution is waiting. You give away your power and empower your partner to control the way you experience the relationship. You focus on trying to find inner integration through external communication and changing your partner. You are trapped in the false belief that your life will change only if the other person changes first. If you then have a verbal exchange with your partner, it will be at a superficial level, and you will not change.

The Open Window

When I first moved into the ashram, I felt like a new-comer, insecure and uncomfortable among the residents. Looking at the disciples who had been living together a long time, I felt very separate. There was such obvious love flowing between them, such companionship and bonded-ness. Everyone seemed to be old buddies. Where did I fit in?

In the face of such family togetherness, I pulled away. My feelings of separateness grew until I felt quite isolated.

Evening satsanga in those days was held in a large barn at our newly acquired ashram in Summit Station, Pennsyl-vania. One evening I decided to share my feelings of loneli-ness with Gurudev. "Gurudev," I said, "I don't feel that I'm fully part of what's going on here. I see love, but I don't feel included in that love."

Gurudev answered, "Love is shining all around you like the sun on a clear day. But you're the one who has to open your own doors and windows in order to receive it. Love can't come to you until you open up to it."

Sitting before Gurudev in the stillness that followed, my attention was drawn upward. Directly above him was a big, wooden window, shuttered tight. As I looked at it, I had an internal experience: I saw myself opening the shutter and imagined light pouring in, covering me with warmth.

In that instant I realized that I couldn't wait for friendship to come to me—I needed to initiate relationships.

In the weeks that followed, my entire attitude in being with people shifted. I took risks to begin conversations. I started reaching out, actively offering my friendship to others. I no longer waited for love to come to me; I offered my own, and therefore received love in return. The window inside my heart had opened.

— *DEVANAND*

TOGETHER

Everything you do after birth
has one purpose:
to lead you toward the second birth,
your spiritual rebirth.

That is the quest of the soul.

Marriage carries that deep purpose,
that evolutionary urge, within it.

Attune your marriage to that search—
to freedom from attachments and fears.

Keep your heart free to love the other
through the ever-expanding love
of the Higher Self within.

Allow your union to support
your path, your inner journey
toward the strength
that lies hidden inside you.

Nurture not only yourself but the other.

Know the other
is the very extension of yourself.

Together follow the path
within you.

To stop blaming, first admit that your experience with another person is always a function of your emotional and mental climate, which was already in place. Nobody has the power to create within you something that is not already there. Whatever you are feeling in a relationship existed already within you.

After owning your part, acknowledge that the way someone treats you has nothing to do with you. Each person is acting for his own reasons, out of his fears, needs, history, and feelings. If you truly understand and accept that, your reactions simply fade away. They disintegrate with the awareness that your lovability and self-worth have nothing to do with another's behavior. When you practice such clarity, you find yourself suddenly able to accept others, regardless of the ways they may have manifested their humanness in conflict with you.

Remember that your relationships provide the potential for everything you have avoided about yourself to be brought to the surface for examination and healing. While your partner doesn't cause the feelings and fears you are experiencing, he does serve one vital purpose: surfacing what is inside you waiting to be faced. Through intimacy and vulnerability with your partner, you can bring an end to the denial and protectiveness that have concealed the feelings hidden inside you. You have an opportunity to deal consciously with what has been unconscious.

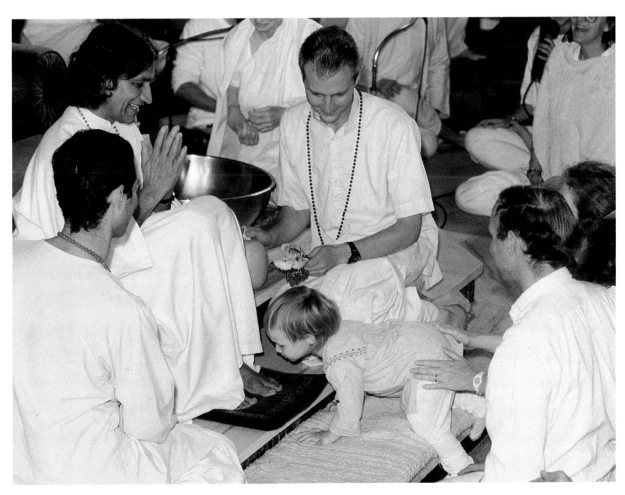

Relationships are what I call a "therapeutic irritation." The moment something from your unconscious surfaces in an interaction, you have a choice. You can either deal consciously with what you are seeing or push it back into your unconscious and leave it there to surface again, when it may feel even more difficult to digest because you avoided it earlier. Whatever you suppress from fear of pain, your life will again and again bring to the surface for you to deal with consciously. When you are conscious, you make it a therapeutic process, a healing, and a sadhana. If you avoid facing what comes up, you simply go on living in conflict and inner pain.

When conflict arises in a relationship and your undigested feelings and history surface, go to the aspect of yourself that is filtering your perception in the moment. Take time with yourself to meditate, walk, or just be quiet, and identify the filter you are placing on the situation. As you identify the filter, you will see where it first was formed, either in your history with your partner or elsewhere in your life.

With that understanding, you will recognize how the filter blocks your ability to be fully present with your partner, prevents you from accepting the situation that is taking place, and keeps you from seeing the truth about yourself. What you

---

Beautiful Sister

Both my younger sister Kunti and I have lived in the ashram for many years. She's a genuinely beautiful person, with a most upbeat, cheerful heart and soul. People love to be around her because of the bright light that shines in her.

One day I was describing her to Gurudev, telling him all the qualities I love about her. I was saying to him, "Gurudev, she's such a beautiful person and . . . "

He stopped me in mid-sentence, looked deeply into me, and said, "And so is my daughter, Chitra."

Gurudev knew that in that moment I was comparing myself to my sister and finding myself lacking. He sensed it, without any word from me, and he was *not* going to let any moment, any opportunity, go by without inviting me back to a focus of self-acceptance. He knew that if I didn't have a foundation of self-love, I couldn't really grow. I couldn't even love my sister fully, because love for another can never go deeper than our love for ourselves.

Gurudev never misses an opportunity to show others their beautiful characteristics. I'll never forget that moment with him, a moment that took me home to myself. Now when I think about my sister and all her beautiful qualities, I always think, "And so is my daughter, Chitra."

— CHITRA

recognize, you can change. When you use a relationship to let go of your past concepts, the relationship becomes transformative for you: it transcends the form of your conceptual framework around the way a relationship should be.

Through conscious immersion in your inner process, you open an enormous possibility between you and your partner. If, through the filter of your fears, his expression has appeared angry, now, without your fear, you see that expression in a different way. Behind the angry expression, you see *his* reality going on, the reality that you formerly were blind to because you were dominated by fear and filtering.

Your whole understanding of what is really going on shifts. You accept your partner more, and respond to his deeper feelings: the insecurity, fear, or uncertainty behind what you once viewed solely as anger. Then you can facilitate real communication and change. As you reopen your heart to your partner, he has the opportunity to respond to the acceptance and clarity coming from you.

By working only on yourself in relationship, you return to your source, the center within you from which true love flows. When your heart center is thus opened, your behavior is unified and genuinely loving.

Your capacity to accept and love the other is like a flower. When the flower blooms, it passes its fragrance on to whoever is present to receive it. Your love then flows from your inner source, not from your fantasies about your partner.

Through your conscious presence and your focus in the eternal now, you transform yourself and expand your capacity to love your partner more fully. By using your relationship as a vehicle for your soul's journey home, you move into the realm of universal love. ◆

135

Real Love

In 1973 I had been married for five years and believed that I knew everything there was to know about being in relationship and being in love. I considered myself an expert—a mature woman with a healthy, committed marriage.

As my husband Michael and I arrived at the Sumneytown ashram, I felt some trepidation. Michael had known the yoga teacher, Amrit Desai, for quite a while and thought very highly of him. I got out of our truck hesitantly, feeling a little jealous and very uncomfortable. I didn't know what to expect from this man Amrit. Then I saw somebody running down the path in sneakers, a black pony tail, and a bandana headband. It was Amrit. Michael followed him into the house while I trailed behind, letting Michael take the lead.

Inside, I stood back and watched Michael face Amrit. I remember the room and their faces in unbelievable clarity and detail, even though twenty years have passed. It felt like the first time I had ever really opened my eyes. In an instant, I saw all the things I have since heard Gurudev teach over the years about discipleship and love. The reality of Amrit's love felt as clear to me as the particles of sunlight flooding the room.

In my eyes, Amrit was only Michael's yoga teacher. I was the one who had been Michael's true love for five years. And yet here was Amrit looking at Michael with a level of love I had never experienced. I realized that I didn't have the foggiest notion of real love, because here it was in front of me for the first time.

In that moment I was awakened to the possibilities of a love bigger than I had ever known, a love larger than my concepts about it. I stood back and observed the moment, feeling my face soften, feeling my mind dissolve into my inner center. This man with the huge brown eyes smiled at my husband, then turned to me and said so sweetly, "Oh, you're Michael's wife. How wonderful." That was the beginning of my journey with Michael on the road to discovering the nature of real love.

— *GAURI*

Offer your Heart

As you love yourself,
love comes through you.

Offer that love
to everyone
you meet today.

Bring yourself closer
to someone.

Bring someone closer
to you.

As you offer yourself
to someone,
you offer your heart
to yourself.

Love is not
an isolated incident
practiced with
a certain person
during a certain
time of day.

Love is
using every opportunity
to bring someone closer
to your heart.

*Treat each person
as if God has come
to teach you
through that person.
As you learn to be
fully present and accepting
of each person you meet,
you transform yourself.
You learn to embrace
and love the whole universe
through that one person.*

TRANSFORMATION THROUGH WITNESS CONSCIOUSNESS

When you have a negative reaction in the midst of an interaction with another, you have an opportunity to transform yourself. By practicing the principles of Kripalu Yoga, you can release the old fear that is triggering your reaction and expand your understanding of what is really taking place in the situation.

The more you practice what I call "holding an emotional posture," the more you will find that your mental or emotional resistance to any person or situation parallels the experience you have when performing a yoga posture to a level that is just beyond your reach.

When holding a posture, or asana, in yoga, you are confronted by physical blocks that are present in your body. Similarly, in an emotional encounter with another person, you are facing inhibitions present within your psyche. Any emotional suffering you experience is caused by your reacting unconsciously, out of fear. Fear generates struggle and pushes you automatically into an emotional and mental posture of resistance.

How can you release the posture of resistance? First, become fully aware of your reaction, observing all the ways your emotional and mental resistance is being translated into physical sensations. Experience the variety of bodily sensations that arise. Observe the places in your body that tighten in a reaction of armoring or defending. As you observe each tense place, relax it immediately. By resolving the physical tensions, you begin to resolve the emotions causing them.

The Darshan Room

I am dedicated to yoga sadhana and have practiced it several hours each day for many years. In the course of my practice, I once had an energetic experience that stirred up a great deal of sexual energy inside me. I know it is not an uncommon phenomenon for yogis and is discussed in yogic scriptures, but the experience left me feeling a little uncomfortable and I decided to consult Gurudev.

One day I was assisting Gurudev in his workout on the weight machine upstairs in his house. At the end of the session, he turned to me with a smile and said, "How is your sadhana?"

I replied, "It's going well, Gurudev; however, I recently had an energy experience that I'd like to talk to you about at some point." Gurudev was standing there, dressed in a sweat suit. He turned and walked quickly downstairs to his darshan room, and I followed.

I knew he had gone ahead of me so that when I walked into the darshan room I would find him in the role of guru. Gurudev did not want to talk in the stairwell about something so sacred to us as this aspect of sadhana; he wanted to offer me a beautiful experience.

As I entered the darshan room, the guru sat before me. The friend with whom I had just lifted weights was gone, and here sat my yoga master and spiritual teacher. I shifted into the role of disciple and offered my pranams.

Gurudev asked me what was happening, and I shared with him about my unusual sadhana experiences. He smiled the entire time I was speaking. Then he said, "What's happening to you is wonderful. You've come to a beautiful and special place in your growth." His eyes were dancing with delight.

"Gurudev, I'm happy to hear that. What should I do if I have such an experience again?"

He became still, and said, "Let your energy do whatever it wants, and don't try to figure it out with your mind. When the experience you've described happens, invoke my presence. Call on the presence of the guru and surround yourself in the protection of our lineage of masters."

Ever since, whenever I get uncomfortable or frightened, I call on Gurudev. I've realized I can apply that technique in all the areas of my life, not just sadhana. As a result, I feel able to deal with any difficult situation.

All I have to do is call on Gurudev.

— *YOGANAND*

Next, identify your feelings of fear, hurt, or anger, doing so without justifying yourself or criticizing another. Watch how your mind wants either to make someone else responsible for your feelings or to judge you for having a reaction.

Fully and objectively experience all your physical sensations, feelings, and thoughts, as if you were a fascinated observer watching an interesting movie. When you note your responses to a situation without adding the judgements brought on by your concepts about what is good or bad, you are practicing witness consciousness.

So, as you feel all your reactions, drop any judgements you have about them. Don't blame yourself or denounce yourself as a bad person. Self-condemnation adds to the problem caused by your resistance.

Self-judgement locks you into your concepts about the event. Instead, allow yourself to flow in rhythm and harmony with your experience.

Relax and take long deep breaths, just as you do when holding an asana, and melt into the full experience of what is happening within you. Breathing relaxes your mental judgements, calms your emotional reactions, and melts away physical tensing and armoring. It gives you space to evaluate your interpretations of the situation, while avoiding a rash response that could hurt another and give you reason to judge yourself later.

The moment you gracefully recognize your feelings without judging yourself or trying to blame another, you bypass your reactive mode of being and enter a new dimension of clarity. From that perspective, you can discover the true cause of your feelings.

As you breathe deeply, then, place yourself in witness consciousness and ask, "Where is my reaction really coming from?" Deep, slow breathing will help put you in touch with your inner self, where you will see the true source of your resistance. Remember that whatever pain or anger you experience in a here-and-now situation is almost always rooted in an undigested fear from your past that has surfaced now to be healed.

If you allow yourself to experience the fear fully, without trying to push it away, an inner shift takes place that initiates transformation. Where the average person might be feeling frustration and blame, you are using the situation to encounter your unfaced fears and resolve them. You shift from an external drama where you seem a victim of circumstances to your inner world where you have the power

and freedom to change.

See the process as a wonderful game! Nobody will know that you are doing a psychic posture, that you are a yogi practicing an invisible yoga, but through your practice of witness consciousness, you will go beyond your automatic, subjective reactions to a deeper reality. By observing your resistance, holding your inner posture, and passing through the frustrations of the mind, you will recognize that the true source of your reaction is within you. Holding the posture and witnessing enable you to face your deeper fears and transform them automatically.

As you practice holding your inner posture in more and more situations, you will begin to receive the true experience of the moment. You will be in direct interaction with life and reality and, thereby, you will move from the unreal to the real and from the darkness of your fears into the light of consciousness. ◆

144

WITNESS CONSCIOUSNESS

Your consciousness
manifests through your body.

Yet you are not your body.

Your consciousness
manifests through your
thoughts and emotions.

Yet you are not
those thoughts or emotions.

You are the choiceless witness.

Allow all thoughts,
all moods, all emotions
to pass through the vast sky
of your consciousness.

Rise above all changes.

Remain choiceless.

Remain the unwavering observer.

You are the spirit that exists
above the body, above the mind.

Witness the dance
of creation.

Breakthrough

Gurudev has always gone out of his way to support me. He's been there for me as if I were his son.

I came to the ashram with a history of alcoholism. The disease of addiction was in my family and I was deeply affected by it. Once I settled into our Kripalu family, however, I realized that our lifestyle was what I was thirsting for, not alcohol.

Gurudev's unconditional love helped me feel at home and welcome in the community. In spite of my low self-esteem, Gurudev demonstrated that I was lovable exactly as I was. I became sober and remained so for many years.

My life was going well, but then I came to a crisis. My ego wanted to prove that I had control over my addiction. I went out one night with a few friends and ended up drinking. I thought I could have just one drink, but I couldn't. I suffered a relapse and started drinking again while living in the ashram. The relapse brought with it a tremendous amount of self-rejection and pain.

Looking for help, I confided in Krishnapriya, Gurudev's assistant. To support me, she informed Gurudev about my predicament, and he immediately came to my aid.

One night after satsanga, Gurudev called me over to talk with him. He seemed to know exactly what was happening for me. We sat and had a beautiful talk in which I shared with him my story. He listened without judgement or reaction.

He was caring but firm, like a father. He pointed his finger at me lovingly and said, "I want you to come directly to me for help if you ever drink again." He radiated warmth and understanding.

The exact words of our conversation weren't important. What mattered to me was that Gurudev, whom I had sometimes made up to be a shaming authority figure, was completely accepting of my behavior and of me.

Gurudev was the person I loved most in the world, and at first I wanted to hide my imperfections from him. Now he knew the whole story, even intuiting parts of it that I hadn't said. There was nothing for me to hide. Together we brought my shame out into the open to release it. From that night on, my denial about the situation disappeared.

With the cloud of denial and shame lifted, I knew I had the opportunity to make a choice about my life, to accept myself exactly as I am each moment. Gurudev's unconditional acceptance opened up that possibility for me. He provided the safety and the setting in which I could let go of my fears. Alcoholism has not been an issue for me since that night many years ago.

—SATYAJIT

The moment you gracefully recognize your feelings
without judging yourself or trying to blame another,
you bypass your reactive mode of being
and enter a new dimension of clarity.

Harmony And Harmonium

Gurudev provides an extraordinary model of the way to live his teachings. Consistently, he shows me that he lives exactly what he teaches.

A few years ago, my wife and I moved near the Lenox ashram to be part of the Kripalu family. Soon after we arrived there was a celebration at the ashram. It was Guru Purnima, the ancient Indian holiday honoring the guru. I was thrilled and excited, since it was my first chance to see Gurudev since we'd moved.

I wanted to get to the ashram early to get a good seat. It meant a lot to me to sit close to Gurudev on that day to experience the powerful spiritual celebration up close. However, my wife, Shakti, has a reputation for being late, and as we began getting ready, she was living up to it. As it got later and later and she was nowhere near ready to leave, I started getting annoyed with her. I tried hurrying her along, but of course that didn't work at all.

Finally we got into the car. I brought my coffee with me in a traveling mug—fortitude for the twenty minute drive. I was exasperated and anxious and drove quickly toward the ashram. Somehow as we conversed in the car, it came up that one of Shakti's friends had phoned the day before. I had asked the friend to call back later but had forgotten to tell Shakti about it. When Shakti found out, she got quite annoyed with me, because she had been waiting for that particular call.

I got self-righteous. I said to Shakti, "It wasn't necessary for me to tell you since she was going to call you back anyway."

Shakti simply wanted me to admit my mistake, but I refused to acknowledge that I had made one. I got more and more self-righteous, and more and more angry at Shakti. After all, she was making me late to see my guru.

To make matters worse, I proceeded to spill my coffee right down the front of my white pants.

We finally arrived at the ashram and entered the large chapel. It was packed—wall-to-wall bodies, without a seat anywhere—typical of a celebration at Kripalu. I was fuming by then.

Fortunately, one of the disciples we knew saw us and took us to two reserved seats up front. Gurudev hadn't arrived yet and I managed to sit down, trying to compose myself. I was agitated and off-center, consumed by my anger and annoyance at being made late by Shakti.

Gurudev entered the room. His harmonium was brought and he began to chant. Sometimes his chanting is incredibly angelic and sometimes it isn't. On that particular morning he couldn't quite get the chant, and he couldn't seem to connect his voice to the melody. Finally he chanted a phrase. We all tried to respond, but we sounded awful, too.

After a few lines he stopped dead, looked up at us, and said, "Boy, I just can't remember this chant. It's an old chant of Bapuji's that I wanted to do to honor him on Guru Purnima. But I just can't seem to get the tune on the harmonium." Then he smiled and giggled. He began playing the chant again, and this time his playing and chanting were beautiful.

I was amazed by the willingness of this man to admit his mistake in front of six or seven hundred people, on such a special occasion. He was so easy with himself, so real and honest. Whether he was "right" or "wrong," he had no need to separate himself from us in the way I had separated myself from Shakti.

After the darshan was over, Shakti and I looked at each other and started laughing. Our conflict of the morning now seemed insignificant and silly to us both. I told Shakti that though I had been unwilling earlier to acknowledge my mistake, I could do so now. I was deeply inspired by Gurudev's willingness, courage, and humility to admit his mistake, and thus inspired found it easy to apologize to my wife.

And that's the way Gurudev has always taught me—by the way he lives. By the subtle, little, off-the-cuff things he does, Gurudev routinely demonstrates his teachings through his actions.

— VASUDEV

149

RESPONDING TO ANGER
A Satsanga Sharing with Gurudev

I have a very painful situation with my sister that I haven't been able to resolve. She seems angry most of the time. Ninety percent of her words to me come out in an angry way. No matter what I do, I just can't make her stop being so angry. This has gone on for a long time, and I'm afraid I'll have to spend the rest of my life dealing with her anger. What can I do?

GURUDEV: The first step is not to resist the fact that anger is present. Then embrace the situation as an opportunity for you to work out your karma. Don't think it is negative to have this conflict going on with your sister. It has a place in your evolution, and it's a perfect invitation for you to handle unresolved karma within you.

Life gives us only as great a dose of karma as we are capable of digesting. But a digestible dose will feel undigestible if you resist a situation instead of using it productively to work on yourself.

Realize that your experience with your sister is co-created. She is not capable of making you feel something that doesn't exist inside you. When she gets angry, she's pushing your buttons, and that triggers your emotional reaction. When she is angry and you react to her anger, she is pushing you against the wall of your fear of anger.

You see, it is not her anger that confronts you; it is your fear of anger. The fear is yours, even though the anger is coming from her. You interpret her anger through the filter of your fear. If you learn to let go of your fear, her anger will lose the power that your fear is projecting onto it.

151

So, don't resent her for your experience of fear either. Realize that it is an old fear hidden inside you, and she is simply the catalyst bringing it forth.

Stay present in the experience that is happening in the reality of the moment. Don't go into the past and dwell on how often she's been angry with you; neither think about the future, imagining that her anger will go on forever. If you do either, you're tackling your entire life, and her anger and your reaction are only happening now. If you dwell on past hurts or future fears, you'll feel helpless and impotent when she gets angry, and you won't feel the power to face your fear.

How do I know whether what's happening is resulting from my fear or just her anger?

GURUDEV: Focus your attention on what you are doing within you, not on what she is doing to you. Yours is a common reaction in relationship—wanting the other to change so you will feel more comfortable. Your sister can never change your karmic response of fear simply by adjusting her angry expression. Only you can resolve your fears.

What can I do to work through my fear when she gets angry?

GURUDEV: First, take a deep breath before you mechanically react out of fear. Use your breath to center and relax. Breathing gives you an opportunity to become more conscious and stops your negative reaction from complicating the interaction. It puts a little separation between you and your emotions, and calms the defensive energy that springs up. Then there is a greater chance for you to be fully present and open to the moment.

Remember that you are not an ordinary person; you are a spiritual seeker. You have discovered new ways to be in life that are inaccessible to most people.

152

At that point, look beyond the anger and see who your sister really is and what she needs in the moment. Probably she wants more love. She may imagine that you are not loving and supporting her or maybe a childhood fear of her own is coming up, and you are triggering something in her. See the situation from her side, and create space for her to have her fears, just as you are having yours. Then you can view her with compassion instead of blame.

Put the incident in the proper perspective. Don't generalize about her behavior, telling yourself she *always* acts this way and that it will *never* end. Consciously recall her love and intention to love you as she has expressed it in the past. Dwell on your appreciation; that keeps the current conflict in its proper perspective.

Sometimes that's hard for me to do.

GURUDEV: It is not always easy, but doing so will create the opportunity for the most open and loving dialogue possible between you, so that you can both use the situation for your growth.

Think of what will encourage her to feel safe and open with you. Angry people are often feeling fearful and threatened underneath their angry expression, and love diminishes both anger and fear. Rather than condemn her, make her feel safer and more comfortable in every possible way. If you are considerate and loving, providing whatever makes her feel valued, you create an opening for your sister to want a loving dialogue with you. By recognizing her needs and responding to them, you open the way to communication and resolution.

153

Pray for your sister—meditate on her—and you will find the appropriate way to give to her so that she can accept your love. When you pray for her and fully accept her in your heart, you are contacting God in the form of your sister. God comes to you through your relationships. God is giving you an opportunity to look beyond the form of an angry sister to see the deeper truth taking place, both about her anger and your fears.

But when she's angry I can't talk to her.

GURUDEV: Wait until both of you are feeling quiet and open, then dialogue about your feelings. Let yourself be the first to admit, in a non-blaming way, which of your fears are active. Be open and reveal your vulnerable side. Tell her what you are learning about yourself. Tell her about your intention to have a loving relationship with her. When she responds, listen openly, even if at first she is blaming or unclear. Your intention is to open a dialogue, not to prove a point or be right. She needs to feel that you care about and understand her point of view. Your understanding will open her up to understand you.

Sometimes I wonder, Gurudev, why I must always be the one to reach out first?

GURUDEV: You are the one to reach out because you are the one who recognizes it as an opportunity to change your inner life and transform your fear. Remember that you are not an ordinary person; you are a spiritual seeker. You have discovered new ways to be in life that are inaccessible to most people. Use your experience of conflict to practice being a seeker, to face your fears about anger, and to bless your sister by loving her even more and praying for her.

If you practice what I've told you, you will see a miracle take place in your relationship with your sister and in yourself. She may still get angry, but you will not get as hooked into your fears. As a result, you will be able to accept and love her more fully, and she will feel safe and received. In that way, you will help her drop her anger.

What is even more important for you, though, is that you will be accepting the invitation from life to face the fear inside you, and in facing it, you will free yourself to live in joy and happiness. ◆

Life gives us only as great a dose of karma as we are capable of digesting.

Jake Meets Gurudev

Years ago at the Sumneytown ashram, I lived in an old stone building called Ananda Kutir, while all the other residents slept in dormitories on a distant part of the property.

At two o'clock one morning I was awakened from a deep sleep by commotion and noise downstairs. I stumbled sleepily down the stairs, fumbled for the light switch, and found myself face to face with a large man—well over six feet tall—whom I had never seen before. I was surprised and a bit scared, but managed to say, "Who are you?" He bellowed at me, "I'm Jake, who the hell are you?" Jake was obviously in a rage.

I tried to talk to him, but he made sense in one moment and no sense in the next. He said that his girlfriend had abandoned him to come to the ashram, that he had just left a mental institution to find her, and that he wanted to see Gurudev right away. His mood shifted from agitated gruffness to violence, and back again.

When I tried to calm him, he got even more riled up and said to me, "I'm going to put your head through that stone wall if you don't take me to Gurudev—now!" Although I was frightened for myself, my focus became protecting Gurudev from Jake's anger. Jake soon forgot about his threat to me and pressed me more as to the whereabouts of Gurudev.

Telling Jake that I had to make a phone call to arrange his meeting with Gurudev, I left the room and anxiously called two other residents. The brothers came quickly and I was relieved to have them with me. The three of us took Jake to my room upstairs to continue talking—or rather listening—to Jake, who was still in a state of semi-controlled rage. At no point was his conversation rational.

Suddenly Jake jumped up, grabbed a large picture of Gurudev from my altar, and smashed it on the floor, shattering glass everywhere. He screamed "I'll get him!" and ran blindly out of the building. The three of us, startled and confused, followed him to another building, which he ran around several times before smashing some of its windows.

Several hours had now passed since I first met Jake, and no resolution seemed in sight. I sneaked away from him, called the police, and then called Gurudev at Muktidham, his retreat cabin, to inform him of the situation. Gurudev was in the middle of meditative seclusion, a period during which he was in solitude, but I felt the night's circumstances warranted disturbing him.

After I explained the situation to Gurudev, he paused for a few moments, then said, "I'm coming down to meet Jake. Call the police again and tell them not to come." I didn't like his plan. Both his meeting Jake and our calling off the police seemed to me to be dangerous choices. I told Gurudev that, but he was firm. "Please do as I've asked," he said. Gurudev's clarity convinced me and the other brothers, concerned and doubtful though we were, to cancel the police call.

Gurudev left his seclusion in Muktidham and came down to the meditation room in his family's apartment in the main part of the ashram. He called us and told us to bring Jake over to see him. As the three of us were walking Jake to Gurudev's apartment, I felt an uncomfortable conflict between wanting to protect Gurudev and trusting his judgement.

Gurudev came out of the house to meet us. He said hello to Jake, then turned to us and said, "You can go now." We didn't want to leave Jake and Gurudev alone, but we walked away and sat down nearby to wait. About forty-five minutes passed, without any of the

noise, yelling, or commotion that Jake had been creating all night. Finally Gurudev opened the sliding door of his residence and called us over. The three of us walked in and there stood Gurudev and Jake, side by side. Jake had a glowing, warm smile on his face.

I was shocked. Gone was the angry, violent man. Here instead stood a soft, open person. Gurudev explained, "Jake and I talked about the ashram and about life. Jake had a breakthrough. He needs to leave now in order to take care of some unfinished business in his life." Jake stood next to Gurudev with a sheepish, friendly smile on his face.

As we walked Jake to the parking lot, we were amazed by the dramatic reversal in his mood. After he left, we went back to talk to Gurudev. Sitting quietly in his meditation room, Gurudev told us, "When you called me about Jake, I had an immediate vision of hugging him. I visualized Jake's heart opening." From that split-second insight, Gurudev decided to meet with a physically violent, angry man, despite the potential danger to himself. Gurudev believed in his vision and his vision came true.

Gurudev's fearlessness in following his heart showed us that night that pure love can transform any situation. Absolutely anything is possible through love, including the transformation of rage and hostility into tranquility and peace, as we saw right before our eyes. It was an extraordinary privilege for us to witness the change that the power of Gurudev's consciousness can effect.

— *VIVEKANAND*

WIN WITHOUT FIGHTING
A Satsanga Sharing with Gurudev

*G*urudev, you've said that if you fight, you have everything to lose and nothing to gain. Right now I am being sued for divorce by my wife. We are going to court, and I'm struggling to figure out how to be in the process with her.

GURUDEV: Even though you are trying to figure out how to be in this process of divorce with her, you must realize that the situation is not really about dealing with her. It is about how to be with yourself—what goes on within you when someone you care about is apparently trying to hurt you. Only by focusing on your inner process, rather than how to be with her, will you really solve your problem. When you work from that perspective, you can handle the external needs of the situation without fighting.

You see, someone else's fighting actions do not automatically put you in a fighting position. If you are not fighting your wife internally, you can take whatever actions you feel are fair, necessary, and appropriate.

The person who takes the position of a fighter is always feeling guilty or fearful or out of control. He has lost his center and is reacting out of emotion and fear. His life is a constant struggle to be in control, because he has lost trust in the process of life.

Your real problem, then, is the fighter within you, not the external issue of fighting the case. The real case you must handle is your own internal fight.

In the beginning I decided that the best defense would be a good offense. So I took the offensive against her and created a big

Change Of Attitude

When I was an ashram resident, my sadhana was my life. I was an eager, consistent practitioner and sometimes stayed up all night doing yoga postures.

After noticing many of my ashram friends' inconsistent sadhana habits, I spent a week trying to encourage some of them to commit to morning yoga practice, but to no avail: they were more attracted to sleeping late than doing yoga. Frustrated, I gave up on them, judging them as "missing spiritual possibilities," and refocused on my own devotional commitment.

A few days after I stopped my crusade, I walked Gurudev home from satsanga. "I want you to encourage the brothers to do consistent yoga practice," Gurudev told me, knowing of my passionate dedication to sadhana. "Communicate with them according to where they are, rather than where you expect them to be. That's the essence of true communication. Don't be self-righteous about it. Offer them acceptance and love, no matter what their attitude is."

"Well, Gurudev," I said, "your advice is good, but I just spent a week doing exactly that and I feel frustrated because I wasn't able to change anybody's attitude."

Gurudev looked at me and said, "What do you think *I* do?"

In that moment, I realized how consistently Gurudev works year after year to inspire people to do sadhana. I compared my puny, one-week effort to his lifelong commitment to help us make conscious choices and his never-ending efforts to find new ways to inspire us. The realization hit me full force.

After that night, I changed my attitude. I became more patient, supportive, and accepting of people as they are, instead of judging them according to the way I think they should be. Gurudev taught me how to truly support others by first accepting them and then communicating with nonjudgement and love. I have used Gurudev's example as the cornerstone of what is now my career—teaching communications and team-building.

— *PRAPHUL*

whirlwind of motion. After a couple of months of that, I felt exhausted internally and hadn't accomplished anything externally. I finally decided to let things sit for awhile and come to Kripalu to take care of myself.

GURUDEV: Whenever we act in retaliation and aggression to get back at someone we feel has wronged us, we not only fail to achieve anything productive, but we destroy our own peace of mind and clarity. The poisonous seeds of revenge that we plant in anger have to be harvested, and in the end we hurt only ourselves.

You reacted in a completely natural and human way, though, so don't now replace the blame you felt toward your wife with blame for yourself. You came here to resolve the conflict inside you. The first step in that resolution is learning not to hate your wife or fight internally with her even if you believe she is attacking you. Don't justify yourself by making her wrong, and don't create self-blame either, making yourself wrong.

Let your actions be focused on reconciling the conflict between you and your wife, as well as the conflict within you. This situation is teaching you how not to fight what is going on in your experience, and that is a profound secret of life. When you learn that secret, you will never again get into a predicament like this.

Unconditional Love

Gurudev is my father.

When I was eighteen, I went with him to an international conference attended by many world-renowned yogis and teachers. I was there to assist with his program.

Once the conference began, a series of events took place that appeared to involve deliberate slights toward Gurudev. For example, during the opening event, he wasn't introduced from the podium with the other yogis, even though he was slated to be one of the keynote speakers and principal teachers. Dad said nothing about it, but I was disappointed and confused.

I found out that my dad's teaching time was only half as long as that of other teachers, scheduled for very early in the morning, and located in a distant, obscure building. I felt even more edgy and uncomfortable.

Several similar facts came to light and I began to feel quite upset. Others at the conference told me that internal politics were at work, that because my father had been so well received at the previous year's conference, pressure had been applied to underplay his presence at this one.

I reacted with fury, the proud daughter wanting respect for her dad. I paced back and forth in his hotel room, fuming. "Dad," I said, "how can they do this to you? I'm going to write a letter. Let's leave right now. These people don't deserve to be with you."

I went on and on, incensed at the alleged behavior of the conference organizers. Through my veil of anger, I watched my father sit in calm stillness in a chair in the hotel room, and I shifted into a protective mode. "I'll take care of him," I thought. "I'll make everything okay."

Dad didn't respond to me at all and he showed no interest in joining me in blame and anxiety. Untroubled, he continued to teach each session he was assigned, doing the next thing, going to the next event. To my consternation, he also continued to love the people around him unconditionally, including those I was blaming.

The result was quick, and obvious to everyone. Attitudes toward Gurudev began to change. He received more and more acknowledgement from the organizers. After his first, sparsely attended teaching session, word about him spread. So many people came to his subsequent lectures that new sessions were scheduled in the main hall to accommodate the crowds.

I was amazed at the turn of events. The rest of the conference was an exciting success.

Sitting in the back of the darkened auditorium during the closing event, I thought to myself, "If he had bought into my anger and fear and allowed himself to react, none of this might have happened."

I was moved by my father's ability to love people exactly as they are, whatever their attitude toward him. To me, this is his greatest teaching: unconditional love always has the power to change external events and bring people into harmony and resolution.

— KAMINI

How do I learn that secret?

GURUDEV: No matter what is happening within you or around you, keep asking yourself, "What is my direction in life? Where do I want to go? What will truly solve the problem? How does this experience fit into my spiritual direction?"

Climb out of the quicksand of blame and anger that you were sinking into. Let your energies remain free and accessible for your greater purpose in life—your spiritual growth. Then you won't waste time playing victim, getting angry, or rejecting yourself. Instead you'll create through your clarity a mental spaciousness that provides an opening to explore the depth and vastness of life and all the mysteries it holds.

Don't get hung up in a drama that destroys your peace of mind. Disengaging from your reactions allows the creative forces of consciousness to flow through you and assist your exploration of your human and divine potentials.

Speaking of divine potentials: one of the toughest things about this divorce is that although I've been on this path for five years, and practiced spiritual teachings, I now find myself in a situation of absolute lower consciousness—fighting, blaming, wanting to make her wrong and defend myself. Some yogi!

I keep thinking there was some step I should have taken, somewhere along the road, to avoid this. Part of my struggle is against the reality that I'm in this process at all. I'm trying to find a way out, but there seems to be no way out.

GURUDEV: What you are experiencing is what you believed about yourself— that you are holy—in contrast to what life is revealing to you—that you feel angry and retaliatory. This is a great opportunity to drop your spiritual self-image and align with reality.

By accepting the way you feel about your wife, you gain the facility to work with the situation more effectively. By facing your self-created concepts of a self that is too spiritual to get angry, your real self, which exists beyond all your concepts, can be revealed to you. That is the purpose of the confrontation you're having with your own human nature.

What is emerging from your divorce is what you need to deal with within you. Your wife is only playing a role in refer-ence to a particular event. The feelings you are experiencing surface whenever your expression of life moves to a greater depth, whether in business, a relationship, or any situation you feel deeply invested in. In those major areas of expression, you always encounter the unfinished places within you.

Life actively works to provide balance for you. It aims itself like a heat-seeking missile to search out all the unfaced places within you and bring them to your attention.

The painful events of life provide an opportunity to face yourself and release

No matter what is happening within you or around you, keep asking yourself, "What is my direction in life? Where do I want to go? What will truly solve the problem? How does this experience fit into my spiritual direction?"

the blocks of your hidden fears and feelings. Rather than blame your wife, realize and accept the powerful chance you have to face a part of yourself that she unconsciously exposed through her actions. Then you will not be concerned with winning or losing.

My worst fear isn't losing the case—it's coming away from all this with a lot of bad feelings that will eat me up for years to come.

GURUDEV: Now you're going to the real cause of your conflict. You will never win by taking actions against your wife, because the conflict exists within you. You're in good shape, because this is not about winning or losing, this is about what's happening to you in the process of divorce. Life is attempting to teach you; the divorce is incidental. If you weren't divorcing, you'd be facing the same things inside you through another medium, such as your work.

Where the inner confrontation happens is not the issue. What happens to you and how you process it is what makes the difference in your life. Whether you win or lose the case doesn't really make that much difference, except to your ego.

But what do I do when she keeps hurling one accusation after another at me?

GURUDEV: Accusations come to the person who is defending himself. Accusations stop for the person who is not defending himself. Who then would be the accused? It's so unsatisfying to fight somebody who isn't fighting back. It provides no energy to the accuser. Take the energy out of her accusations by not reacting. Then she'll give up accusing you.

The defensive person provides an ear to hear an accusation where one may not even exist. So much of the accusation we hear comes from our listening with an ear of fear. I realize she may be trying to hurt you in some way, but not all the accusations you are getting are coming from her. Again, it all comes back to your relationship with yourself.

Gurudev, I thank you with all my heart. I appreciate your loving fearlessness in bringing me to the truth. I feel completely different, as though a dark cloud has lifted from my heart. I'm back with myself. ◆

Pearls

We all extract from our relationship with Gurudev what we need most for our growth. Some disciples have been graced by personal experiences with him, others through their connection with guru seva. I have been graced by the power of what I call Gurudev's "pearls," the gems of his teachings. Pithy statements that Gurudev gave years ago still flash in my mind and guide my life. If I never saw or heard him again, what Gurudev has given me through these pearls is enough to practice for the rest of my life.

For example, Gurudev told us once, "Never miss an opportunity to tell people you love them, to tell them they're beautiful, if that's what you feel." Since then, if someone touches my heart, I'll send a little note or phone message to the person, to share my appreciation. I still see Gurudev sitting in front of me, reminding me never to miss an opportunity to appreciate another and to acknowledge love. It's a simple teaching, yet it has changed the quality of my life.

Once I was in conflict and pain about a love relationship I had left when I became an ashram resident. I felt guilty and that I needed to do something to complete with the person. I asked Gurudev what he thought. He said to me, "Sometimes completion comes from our acceptance that the situation is over, and that there is nothing more to do."

From that moment on I let go of any worry or guilt about the relationship and allowed myself to enjoy my life in the ashram fully. I no longer needed to apologize to my ex-lover for my life moving on, or pretend that somehow we were still connected. That freed him as well as me to move on with new lives while graciously honoring the relationship we had shared.

Gurudev gave another pearl to me during a painful time when my first husband and I decided to divorce. I was worried about what Gurudev and my friends would think of me and whether they would accept my decision. Gurudev said, "The question is not whether we will accept you. The question is will *you* accept *yourself?*"

Now when I'm making a decision and trying to figure out how others will judge me, I hear Gurudev asking, "Will *you* accept *yourself?*"

At a darshan for those of us who serve the guests directly, one of the Front Desk staff told Gurudev, "I have a mental list of what I consider to be my job responsibilities as a Front Desk staff person. But every day, guests interrupt to ask things of me that are not on my list, and then I get resentful." Gurudev laughed and said, "That's great! Just think of it: life is like a big Front Desk."

Now, when someone asks me to do something that isn't on my list of responsibilities, I usually find myself saying "yes" anyway. I remember Gurudev's reply that day. Life *is* like a big Front Desk, always teaching me to open to the moment and to the person or situation before me, even if it's not what I had on my list of expectations!

— *RAMESHVARI*

STRENGTH

Your strength is not in your muscles.

It does not come from
fighting negative situations
or winning against a negative enemy.

Your strength is in your calmness,
in the clarity of your mind.

Strength comes from
putting the negative aside,
without reacting.

Win in calmness,
in consciousness,
in balance.

Win without fighting.

Beyond Pleasure To Fulfillment

Everyone seeks happiness and enjoyment from life. The fact is that we need only make a shift in consciousness to find that happiness and enjoyment. Our level of fulfillment doesn't depend on whether we are rich or poor, live in a mansion or a single room, drive a Jaguar or ride a bicycle. What matters is our ability to experience life totally.

The secret to enjoying life lies in our ability to engage ourselves in whatever we do. If we can develop the ability to be one hundred percent total in all our activities, we will feel joyous and alive, and live a highly fulfilled life.

To experience what is happening at any given moment, we must be totally present. Often we go through enormous effort to create pleasurable experiences, yet we forget to develop our ability to take in such experiences. We misplace our attention, ignoring the "experiencer"—ourselves. If the experiencer within us does not cultivate the ability to become passionately absorbed in the moment, then life passes us by.

Having never equals being. No matter what we have, it will never equal the satisfaction we receive from being intently involved in the moment we are experiencing. We seek new experiences because we are hungry for the ecstasy of totality, of being completely present, and we think a new experience will provide us that totality. But newness wears off, so that is not what engenders totality.

The heightened ability to experience, which we seek in new acquisitions and events, actually comes only from full participation in our experience. What enables us to be total is our consciousness, not what we have or what kind of external

experience we engage in. No matter how many experiences we successfully create around us, they all remain outside us.

What keeps us from embracing each instant of our lives and experiencing life deeply? It is our judgements and concepts about what's happening. The criteria by which we judge our experience dictate the way we meet each moment. The conditions we place on how life should appear and feel inhibit our capacity to embrace all of life's richness.

We make a mental list with the titles "Pleasure" and "Pain," and then categorize every moment and experience according to whether it's a pleasurable and therefore desirable experience, or a painful experience to avoid. We cling to the pleasurable experiences and resist the painful ones.

When we are attached to what we call pleasure and resist what we judge as pain, we live in inner conflict and fear. We fear that the pleasurable experience will go away and struggle to keep it. We fear that the painful experience will stay with us and struggle to keep it at bay. Now, instead

Gurudev's Secret

I have worked for Gurudev as his personal assistant for a long time. My seva gives me the unique opportunity to see Gurudev more off the guru's chair than on it; I get to observe him living his life as a man rather than as a guru.

Gurudev loves crystals. He thoroughly enjoys the beauty they offer and delights in displaying them. For a period of time, in an upstairs room in his house, Gurudev placed a favorite folding screen from India and hung long, beaded chains of crystals on it. The display was quite striking.

One day a strong wind blew in and knocked the screen over, breaking quite a few of the crystals. As best as I could, I pieced them back together with glue. However, one of the largest and most exquisite crystals had shattered beyond repair. I was concerned about telling Gurudev, not sure of his reaction.

Later in the afternoon, I was in the kitchen cooking. Gurudev came in and we greeted each other. "Gurudev," I said, "the wind blew your screen down in the upstairs room, and many of your crystals were broken. I was able to fix most of them, but I couldn't fix the largest one."

Gurudev turned and left the room to hang up his shawl. Then he came back into the kitchen, stood in the doorway, and looked me in the eye. He said, "These things are for my pleasure, not my misery." And he walked away. That was it: he was completely finished with the situation.

I realized that much of what I have done in my life has been for my pleasure, yet somehow I have managed to create misery out of it when the pleasurable things are taken away. Gurudev lives in a place of fully enjoying things and situations just the way they are. He doesn't seem to get hooked or attached. He knows how to enjoy things and how to let go.

On another day, Gurudev had just come into the house and we were talking in the small foyer by the coat closet. I took his coat and opened the closet door to hang it up. From my days in the military, I am accustomed to hanging clothes according to length and color, and all facing the same direction. I like things arranged in a neat, organized way, and feel that my energy flows better when my surroundings are in order.

As I hung up Gurudev's coat, I noticed that his son Malay's coat was facing in the opposite direction. I had no personal judgement about it, but, as Gurudev and I continued talking, I took the coat out of the closet, turned it around, and put it back.

Gurudev said, "You are just like me, so orderly."

"Yes," I said, "My energy flows better when things are organized and neat."

I closed the door, said goodbye to Gurudev, and went into the kitchen to begin preparing his meal. Suddenly Gurudev poked his head around the corner and said, "But the secret is not to get disturbed when things are disorganized! Otherwise, you lose the very thing for which you organized them in the first place."

— CHANDRAKANT

Cozy Homes

In 1974, my wife and I were the only married couple living in the ashram. We lived in one room in a building that otherwise housed single ashram residents. While we were very committed to Kripalu, both of us wanted to have our own house, but that was simply not possible in the ashram's early, financially lean days.

One winter evening I was driving Gurudev through a residential part of town on the way to the airport. As we drove, I looked down the street and saw lots of houses with lights on; I could see people watching television and sitting in their living rooms. I thought, "What nice homes. I'd like to live like that. Why don't I have what they do?"

My envious thoughts continued as we drove. Then out of the blue Gurudev said, "Isn't it wonderful that those people have such cozy, warm homes? It's such a wonderful thing to see."

At that time Gurudev, his wife Mataji, and their three children lived in a tiny apartment underneath the meditation room, the busiest part of the ashram. His bedroom doubled as the darshan room where he met with residents during the day, after he and Mataji had rolled up their sleeping mats. Overhead they heard the constant noise of resident activities in the meditation room.

But what Gurudev felt when he saw the cozy homes of others was not envy, but joy for their comfort and security. His simple comment stopped me cold. I saw that my uncomfortable feelings of envy were generated by the way I was looking at the situation. If I changed my attitude, I could change my experience.

I thought to myself, "I could try to see this as Gurudev does." And I did. It was actually quite simple for me to switch my attitude. Only a few weeks later, Gurudev and I were driving together again. This time I was able to look at the passing houses and feel happiness for the people living in them, just as Gurudev did.

Since that ride with Gurudev, I have seldom felt envious of anyone. Gurudev turned me around and showed me how to use the happiness of others to feel good instead. And each time I do that, I know my freedom from envy stems from Gurudev's comment, "Isn't it wonderful that they have such cozy homes?"

— SHANKAR

of the life of joy and pleasure we wanted, we've designed for ourselves an experience of fear and struggle.

The more miserable we become, the more we struggle to push away pain and get more pleasure. We become dominated by the dream of what we don't have and the fantasy of what we'd feel like if we got it. We live in a false hope that one day there will be only pleasure. Then, of course, we'll be happy.

Pain and pleasure, however, are twins; they always come together. If I pick up one end of a stick, the other end invariably comes with it. In the same way, no matter what we pick up in life for pleasure, pain comes along, because once we have a pleasurable experience, we immediately fear losing it. Mistakenly thinking that our joy comes from the thing—or person, or experience—we believe we must now have it always. We become obsessed with keeping available to us what we consider the source of our pleasure. That obsession makes life very painful.

It is sad to see the many people who have invested great energy into acquiring pleasurable experiences rather than developing their ability to experience. If you examine their lives, you will see that frustration and unfulfillment often pursue them. They have become caught in their efforts to create experiences, entangled in their beliefs that external achievements bring fulfillment and happiness. Without an ability to live each moment fully, the deeper secrets of enjoying life remain for them obscure and inaccessible.

Conventional living focuses on external achievements: accomplishing more, acquiring more, and doing more in order to have "the good life." Spiritual life takes you to your source, from which you develop the capacity to experience each moment fully. Spiritual disciplines teach you to develop your consciousness and your ability to accept every moment, so that you may participate fully in the experiences life provides you.

When you receive each experience of your life with openness and receptivity, you deepen your capacity to take life in. As you embrace each moment through unconditional acceptance of its riches, however they appear, life embraces you back, blessing you with feelings of fulfillment, relaxation, and peace.

If you allow life to give you what it chooses, it will reveal to you its profound and loving secrets. When you welcome every experience that comes your way, you receive life's gift of that moment without fear, self-judgement, or resistance. Every experience you have becomes an opportunity for the full scope of reality to reveal itself to you.

Unconditional experiencing of the moment, encountered free of your definitions of pleasure and pain, brings you ultimate freedom, joy, and happiness. The deepest secrets of enjoying life become clear to you as you accept life completely. ◆

The Feast

During my many years of serving as Gurudev's administrative assistant, I have often witnessed the joy he takes in living a simple life.

Gurudev and I were in the heart of downtown Manhattan on ashram legal business. We had driven three hours to the city at dawn and had a busy morning. Now it was lunchtime and I was hungry. We were surrounded by great restaurants.

"Come on, Gurudev," I said, "It's late. Let's find a good restaurant and get some lunch. There are so many wonderful restaurants in this area."

Gurudev was utterly uninterested in finding a restaurant. He said, "No, here, I have lunch. Let's not spend ashram money on a restaurant." He took a brown paper bag out of his briefcase. Typically, Mataji had sent him off with a home-cooked, Indian lunch for his day in the Big Apple. Like two kids, we ate our bag lunch sitting in the back seat of his car, parked on a Manhattan street as well-heeled New Yorkers rushed by to their lunch dates in swanky restaurants. Gurudev was pleased and content with our little picnic.

Gurudev grew up in what I would call a hut, in a rustic village where eating in a restaurant was unheard of; in his adult life he has lived with extreme frugality. He has rarely shown a desire to sample the wares of cosmopolitan life. Unlike most people I know, Gurudev seems to have no feeling of not having acquired or experienced enough in any arena of his life. He is complete with each experience and content with the simplest things.

At the same time, he's not trying to be holy or righteous or make some kind of spiritual point by being "simple." That is just the way he is. He has taught me how to enjoy life by the way he lives it. Everything is enough to Gurudev, and enough is a feast.

— *KRISHNAPRIYA*

FOREVER FREE

That which
we hide from
haunts us.

That which
we run from
reins us.

That which
we avoid
creates a void
in us.

That which
we clutch
has a hold
on us.

But that which
we allow to flow
leaves us
forever free.

EMBRACE THE WHOLE
A Satsanga Sharing with Gurudev

urudev, many years ago a former ashram resident wrote a very critical newspaper article about you. When he later returned to visit, you were completely relaxed and loving with him, treating him as if nothing had happened. It seemed there was no difference in your heart between him and any other disciple you love. How did you receive such critical, negative energy and not feel hurt or want to retaliate?

GURUDEV: To me, people are more than just human beings caught in the frame of behavior they are choosing to act out at any particular time. I see the potential divinity that exists within every person. I choose to believe in the unchanging higher consciousness, not in the temporary, fluctuating human emotions a person is exhibiting at a given moment.

The personality of a human being is not a fixed event; both the personality and the way it manifests are fluid and ever-changing. Negativity is never permanent. It is energy in motion, simply moving on to some other expression. If I judge someone based on how he acts in one moment in time, then I am focusing only on a tiny part of him, not the whole person.

The disciple you mentioned was not negative forever. He does not always dwell in the frame of mind in which he criticizes me. Knowing that, I did not hold him responsible for what he temporarily felt and acted upon when he wrote the article. There were many other times when he did not feel negative, but was very loving and grateful. He didn't only write a critical newspaper article about me and the ashram; while he was living here, he expressed great love and appreciation for me and the ashram. Why would I selectively choose the negative incident

and assume it represents the ultimate truth of his being?

Should I buy into either his criticism, which is passing, or his appreciation, which is also passing? Why not stay fluid with his changing reality and simply acknowledge that his emotional expression was just what he was passing through at that moment? He reacted to a certain set of his mind and emotions that had surfaced according to his karma, personality, and personal perceptions. I have no need to hold him there.

Gurudev, you are describing a beautiful, spiritually holistic way of looking at life and people. How do you operate from that consciousness, seeing everything from a universal perspective, rather than a judgmental, reactive one?

GURUDEV: I know that physically, mentally, and emotionally we are all exactly where we need to be. Everything in the universe is unfolding as it is meant to. If I get stuck with one particular mode of someone's expression, it tells me more about myself than about the other person.

When you do the work of clearing your consciousness, you discover within you the facility to let go of negative events. As you release negativity within, external negative events have a decreasing effect on you. You won't need to use others' temporary negativity to reinforce your own.

Even before that brother apologized to me, I had dropped the entire incident. I was able to drop it because I have worked to clear my heart of impurities, so that my

178

I know that every individual in my life reveals a part of me that I need to encounter and serves as a medium through which I can see myself, grow in awareness, and come closer to God within me.

compassion may take precedence over my judging mind.

How have you cleared your heart of impurities, Gurudev?

GURUDEV: Constant observation of life purifies the heart. I observe what motivates my behavior when I am wanting to blame and react. I observe the effect that others' blame and reactivity have on their ability to feel peaceful, be conscious, and have clear relationships with others. Observing the truth of what is really going on allows me to make conscious choices about how I respond. I am then able to feel and behave in ways that bring harmony and clarity, rather than blame and upset.

Sometimes I have an immediate emotional reaction, and I am tempted to judge someone or find fault. When that happens, I remember that everything that happens to me, even if it appears to be coming from the outside, is ultimately my own doing. No person or situation in this world ever enters my experience independent of my filters.

Realizing that I create my experience helps me drop my immediate, human reaction and look within me to see why I am having that particular reaction. I see what it is within me that has been activated by a person or event, and I use the situation to expand and clarify my consciousness. That is how I process my emotions internally when a difficult event occurs in my life.

I know that every individual in my life reveals a part of me that I need to encounter and serves as a medium through which I can see myself, grow in awareness, and come closer to God within me. Attuning to higher consciousness rather than to my reactive, changing emotions grounds me in a nonattached, all-embracing, universal outlook.

Is it ever healthy just to blow off steam by reacting emotionally when you are upset with someone?

GURUDEV: If you feel a lot of anger, pain, or fear about a situation, you may need to release those emotions, just to clear them out of your body and mind. If you need to do that, scream into a pillow, pound a bed, cry, or release your feelings in some other therapeutic way. Do it alone, though, or with an objective, supportive friend who understands your need to release and will not be biased by your emoting about the other person.

The key is not to unload your karmic, emotional reaction on the person with whom you are upset. If you can release your pent-up emotions only as a preliminary step toward seeing the whole situation consciously, then you are using conflict to achieve inner freedom.

People build up a karmic history in their lives by misperceiving situations, drawing false conclusions about what those situations mean, and then acting on the mistaken conclusions. With every repeated action based on their own misperceptions, they add to the burden of karma, a burden that creates enormous misery in their lives.

You do not have to be trapped in self-created karma. You have the power to alter your karma through your consciousness. You can transform negative karma into positive energy by using your immediate internal reactions as opportunities to grow in self-awareness. If you stay conscious in handling your reactions, your karmic debt gets paid off a little more each time, and as that debt decreases, your internal freedom grows.

Inner freedom comes from embracing the whole, unconditionally. As you grow spiritually, you embrace more and more of your life experience without reaction or denial. In that embracing, you enter into cosmic consciousness, where you realize that everything in the cosmos is occurring perfectly.

There is nothing, including a painful or upsetting event with another person, that exists outside divine perfection. If an experience were not necessary, it would not happen; it occurs because it is

necessary for your growth. When you come to that awareness, you surrender to what is. You are then able to live in the state of "Thy will be done, Lord, not mine."

But Gurudev, when that brother wrote the article, didn't he actually want to hurt and discredit you? It seems to me you weren't filtering the situation or imagining it; he wanted to bring pain to you.

GURUDEV: Where you saw a man who was apparently trying to hurt and discredit me, I saw a part of myself being revealed through him, in order to bring me closer to God. He gave me an opportunity to be conscious by keeping my vision clearly focused on the reality taking place. By treating him consciously, I further awakened my own consciousness. If I had reacted and treated him unconsciously, I would have fed my unconsciousness.

Some people, seeing my openness in situations like the one with that brother, think that I am very forgiving. It is not forgiveness that I have; it is knowingness. Who am I to forgive anyone? That notion is an affront to the divine perfection of the universe. There is nothing to forgive; there are simply events that take place to teach us and help us to grow. If I feel hurt by someone, my hurt is a function of my own interpretation. If I let go of my interpretation, what is there to forgive?

When someone clearly intends to hurt you, though, shouldn't he take responsibility for his actions?

GURUDEV: What someone else does with a situation is not my territory to be concerned about.

Even if he is clearly wrong?

180

Beyond Anger

After living at the ashram for a few months, I found myself going through many mood swings. Everything about ashram life was new to me and I was having a hard time adjusting to it. One day I was on a ladder painting our main building. The painting was not going well and I was becoming irritated and angry.

About mid-morning Gurudev approached and suggested several ways to improve the painting. That angered me even more. "Who is this guy," I thought, "telling me what to do? What am I doing on this ladder? Why am I working at this place anyway?"

I twisted my head around to look at him, furious by that time. I glared down at him, directing all my fury at him. But a funny thing happened— Gurudev didn't bat an eye. He looked right through my anger, as though he saw only my underlying fear. I'd never in my life experienced anyone staying present with me as I felt such intense feelings. Gurudev did.

Though our interaction was brief, in that short time it was as if he dispelled my negative feelings completely. My anger and tension disappeared. Neither of us said a word. He just walked away and I turned back to my painting.

I realized then that I had found a person who could accept everything I am, someone who could handle even the parts of me that I feared. That incident happened twenty years ago. Since then I have allowed myself to explore the places within where I've stored fear and tension and anger. Gradually, those feelings have been replaced with love and self-acceptance. It all started that day on the ladder.

— NIJANAND

GURUDEV: You never need to be concerned about whether another person is right or wrong. The moment you start evaluating right and wrong, you begin perceiving the other through your filters, and all you see is based on guesswork and speculation. Then nothing gets resolved.

If you turn your attention inward to yourself and your consciousness, you have a possibility of finding out the truth of a situation. By focusing inward, you conserve your energy instead of diffusing and wasting it in blame and judgement. And you need your energy available in order to see yourself—*all* your energy!

No matter what someone does to me, I know I have absolute responsibility for how I feel as a result of his actions. What another person says about me and how other people listen to him are totally out of my control. If I attend to the way I react to his words and actions, everything else is insignificant.

How is it that you can invest so much of yourself in loving someone and remain so non-attached to how you are treated in return?

GURUDEV: I never think about my disciples in terms of how much I have invested in them. What I have done for someone else makes no difference at all. I do not give my love to others with expectations.

A cloud does not invest in the land it showers upon. The cloud showers and then is suddenly nonexistent, as far as the land is concerned. The land may grow a crop or do nothing. It does not matter to the cloud; the cloud has moved on. The shower it gave to the land was a moment that passed. Imagine if the cloud said, "Wow! I gave such a good rainfall to that field. Now I hear it is all dried up. What a waste of time for me to rain there! What an ungrateful field!"

Similarly, I am free of wanting respect or love from the disciples I have served or loved on our mutual journey. That was then; this is now. I have moved on.

As a guru, I may be in a particular role, but I am clear that I am not doing anyone any favors. What a disciple takes from my teachings and love is not my concern or problem. Who am I to take credit? Who am I to take blame? What disciples do is a function of their own choice and

consciousness, and the karma they are actively working with in their spiritual journey. How I am with them is a function of *my* consciousness. I carry no notion that I am giving great things to people.

How did you learn all this, Gurudev? You have never studied psychology and Bapuji never taught you this kind of thing.

GURUDEV: I learn from being in touch with life with endless fascination. I never get tired of observing life, because it is so revitalizing! What I am is the product of the consciousness I have endeavored to develop throughout my life. I haven't studied psychology nor have I formally studied the classical scriptures, but I have been deeply in touch with the scripture that is life. Life teaches me so much more than any book. ◆

Acceptance

For several years, one of my seva responsibilities was arranging Gurudev's transportation to and from local airports when he traveled.

Once Gurudev was returning from a seminar at eleven-thirty on the night before he was to lead an initiation ceremony at Shadowbrook at five o'clock in the morning. I had arranged for two disciples to meet his plane at JFK airport in New York City. The plan was for him to sleep in the car as they drove home. Although I was concerned about his late arrival coupled with his early morning responsibilities, I felt satisfied when I went to sleep that the details were well organized.

My ringing telephone woke me from a deep sleep. I peered through the dark at my clock and saw that it was midnight. "Who could be calling me at this hour?" I wondered, as I groped for the telephone.

"Yes?" I managed, half-asleep.

"Jai Bhagwan. This is Gurudev." His voice brought me out of sleep instantly. "Nobody is here to pick me up yet. Is someone coming?" Although I could tell he was tired after his many hours of traveling and waiting, there was no blame in his voice.

I managed to get the person who had scheduled Gurudev's itinerary on the phone with us, and the three of us pieced together what had happened. With a shock, I realized that while I had sent two disciples to JFK, Gurudev had landed in Hartford, Connecticut.

I felt horrible about my mistake. Here was Gurudev, after hours of travel, sitting in Hartford in the middle of the night without a ride, while a hundred people were to be initiated by him into discipleship in only five hours. Meanwhile, two disciples were wandering around JFK looking for him. And it was all my fault.

When I told Gurudev about my mistake and started to apologize, his focus turned completely toward loving and supporting me. He told me not to worry, that everything would be fine. He was more concerned that I not feel guilty than he was with the inconvenience or the possibility he'd be tired the next day.

We decided that the best plan was for Gurudev to take a cab home, so he could get some sleep before the ceremony. But when I saw him the next day, he told me that he'd taken a bus instead, in order to save the ashram's money! Nevertheless, he was his usual bright, joyful, and present self as he led the three-hour ceremony. He never mentioned the incident to me again and he never lost faith in my ability to take care of details for him.

Through that experience I felt I'd received a personal teaching from Gurudev: "Practice self-acceptance. Nothing is worth rejecting yourself for." The gift of that lesson outweighed the guilt I felt, and I was able to feel good about myself at the same time that I felt regret about my mistake. Gurudev's loving acceptance in the face of my blunder was a turning point for me in my practice of self-acceptance.

— *NILIMA*

PASSIONATE NONATTACHMENT
A Satsanga Sharing with Gurudev

Yogah karmasu kaushalam.
"Yoga is perfection in action."

*H*ow can you perform every action in such a total way that nothing is left over when you have finished—so that nothing within you is left feeling unsatisfied ("I wish I'd had a different experience"), incomplete ("I wish I had more of that experience"), or regretful ("I wish I had handled that differently")? When you live every experience fully, you will never feel dissatisfied about your life.

When you leave an activity half-finished, or live through it halfheartedly, with hesitation and self-doubt, you leave unfinished business that becomes part of your unconscious. That unfinished business is called karma. The consequences of karma, or incomplete experience, must be dealt with sometime in your future.

If, however, you live each experience fully, there will be nothing unfinished about any moment. There will be nothing left to be gained from any experience—nothing left to get out of it.

Gurudev, in the last couple of years I've been feeling a lack of passion for my work. For years I was intensely interested in everything I did, because I had many dreams of what I would get out of it and how I would feel at the end. So I've done many things in my life: led seminars all over the country, written books, developed as an artist, had a successful counseling practice. I've done all the things I wanted to do and I've done them well. I was very passionate about achieving them.

185

Now I've come to a place where nothing turns me on anymore. I've been feeling as though there isn't anything I can do that really feels important. What difference has it all made?

GURUDEV: You have come to a real clarity about life.

But I feel a huge loss of drive. I have to earn a living and make choices about what to do with my time and my work. How do I decide what work to do and set goals and take action when I no longer get a big hit from what I'm doing?

GURUDEV: For most people, the drive and passion they feel in their performance is motivated by dreams they hold for themselves. They fan their passion by making the dreams very attractive and enticing. They project lots of ideas of how it will all be and add fantasies to their dreams. They call these dreams their aspirations and goals—sometimes even their spiritual goals.

Anything that is projected into the future, no matter what you call it, is an escape from reality. Almost everybody reaches the state you are in, but most people are not willing to acknowledge it because they are so heavily invested in the culture and the concepts about "making it" that are so prevalent and hypnotic in our society. It is very difficult to let go of those concepts and acknowledge what you're feeling, as you are doing.

186

To me, it does not matter what I am doing. It's how I am doing it. . . . My attention is on my consciousness, not on having a project turn out the way my mind expects.

Your teachings have helped me realize the difference between my concepts and my real feelings. Now that I've achieved so much that I wanted, I just feel kind of blah about everything. There's a gnawing ache that says I should be doing something different, but I don't want to hop from thing to thing, looking for happiness. I really see that none of what I possess, or have done, has anything to do with how I'm experiencing each day of my life. Nothing.

GURUDEV: So you have learned. You had a need to play out certain experiences in your life and see, once and for all, what it really meant. You went out into the world, experienced all you needed to, and came to the realization that there is more to life.

Now, you must realize what your life is bringing you to, and support your realizations consciously and willfully. You must follow a right course of action, otherwise you will flounder in indecision and unclarity. Indecision indicates you are not acknowledging what you want at the deepest level. You've been acting in habitual, established ways for so long that there is a conflict between what you have been doing and what your soul is calling for. You need to support and acknowledge

what is coming to you from the depth of your life experience.

Right. But meanwhile I have a career to carry on.

GURUDEV: Yes. The passion must come forth through what you are already doing, but with a foundation different from before. It is possible to live with passionate non-attachment. The combination of passion and nonattachment is unique: you need both.

There are two kinds of passion. There is the usual passion that comes from attachment to a goal that is created as a reaction to a problem you imagine you have, a deficiency of some kind. It derives from a basic misperception that you are not enough as you are. From that misperception, you create an external goal you think will satisfy you. You can generate enormous passion in that way, tremendous energy and drive. You will ultimately be disappointed, however, because even when you achieve your external goal, your feeling of incompleteness will still be with you.

The deeper passion comes from a profound love for what you are doing. It doesn't really matter *what* you are doing,

187

Call Him

Gurudev lives in an expanded state of consciousness. I have learned to tap into that consciousness by practicing the presence of the guru in all kinds of situations.

For the thirteen years I lived in the ashram I was fully engaged in the Kripalu life-style and teachings. My life was quite simple, my clothes mostly second-hand. Everything I owned could fit in a few cardboard boxes. Within the rarified atmosphere of the ashram it was natural to draw on Gurudev's presence and wisdom in my seva of leading Kripalu programs.

Several years ago my husband and I decided to leave the ashram and live nearby, to give a different external expression to our lives while still being connected to Kripalu and Gurudev. We started a corporate consulting company, working with high-level executives from multimillion-dollar corporations. After years of simple ashram living I found myself immersed in a radically different lifestyle, sitting in elegant boardrooms serving executives and CEO's who made six-figure salaries.

Initially I felt intimidated, thinking, "What do I have to offer these men with Harvard MBA's? They've been running these companies for years." Then I realized that of the many consultants they had met, they selected us. Why? I believe that on some level our clients feel the consciousness and energy Gurudev represents, which we have practiced and learned from him to express to others.

Training techniques and organizational approaches all have a role in corporate transformation, but I have found that what truly produces breakthroughs are the very qualities Gurudev taught me and modeled. By drawing on his state of being, visualizing him and calling on his guidance, I have been able to do my new "seva" from a level of consciousness greater than that produced through my personal effort and will.

When I practice Gurudev's presence, any limiting thoughts or fears I have about consulting or training situations disappear. My clients are affected too. They often express deep personal feelings they have never felt safe to disclose before. Team members share genuine care and appreciation for each other, while healing old resentments. The power of the guru's consciousness that I tap into, so apparent in every Kripalu program, is just as potent in the corporate world.

Often before a training I meditate for a few moments, clearing my ego out of the way so Gurudev's consciousness can flow through me. I ask Gurudev to bless and help everyone present. Sitting there in a business suit, I pray, "Gurudev, please show me how to listen to these people as you would listen. Help me feel the truth of this situation with my heart. Speak through me as I teach and let your truth and clarity surround this meeting." What then occurs often surpasses what I in my limiting concepts had thought possible for the group to achieve.

Gurudev's energy is universal. What he offers is not contained by a form of ashram, yoga, or spiritual beliefs. He is the living representation of Kripalu: the compassionate, truthful, loving energy that has been transforming people's lives on this path for thousands of years. His consciousness dissolves all boundaries and touches everyone who comes in contact with him, whether directly, or energetically through his disciples.

— SUKANYA

so long as you are totally present and engaged every moment you are doing it.

We derive the greatest pleasure and fulfillment when all our faculties are drawn into our activities. We unconsciously seek activities that most fully engage our minds, emotions, and energies. In the state of absorption, we experience extraordinary satisfaction, so the experience of intense involvement attracts us.

The secret is not to chase after external goals and activities that you think will engage your energies in this way, because the level of pleasure and absorption you get from any activity constantly fluctuates according to your state of mind. There is no external stimulus that consistently gives you the experience of absorption and pleasure; what matters is your consciousness, rather than the medium through which you are acting.

To me, it does not matter what I am doing. It's *how* I am doing it. Concentrating on how I am doing something makes *me* the center of focus. You can see that I'm very passionate about everything I do, yet I can instantly drop any project or experience I have been pouring myself into, because I have no personal attachment to it. My attention is on my consciousness, not on having a project turn out the way my mind expects.

If I concentrate on *what* I am doing, I place my focus on external events and become hooked into needing those events to turn out a certain way. I've then set myself up to get frustrated, disappointed, upset, and out of my moment. By concentrating on what I do, I center my life on external goals at the expense of my inner process.

When you focus on external achievements, you are never satisfied because there is always more to be achieved. Even if you possess the assets of a rich man, there is more to acquire. There is no end to it.

True satisfaction comes from a deeper level of consciousness where doing in itself becomes intrinsically fulfilling. Then you are not basing your satisfaction on the carrot at the end of the stick, but are fully engaged in each step of the journey.

By concentrating on *how* you do something, you become the creator of your experience, rather than having your experience run you. And you create the experience you want immediately, instead of creating external conditions that you think will give you, sometime in the future, the experience you are seeking.

If you think your fulfillment comes from having things, doing things, and being something, you become very goal-oriented and driven. Whenever you are motivated by a goal, you may have great passion and involvement in what you do, but you are living in a dream of the future that takes you away from reality.

Everybody tries to escape reality. Dreams become a tranquilizer to ease the pain of a moment that fails to meet our anticipations. When such escape becomes habitual, we are addicted. Some escapes are visible, others not so visible. Some people use sex,

Corporate Puja

It's easy for me to get caught up in the form of spirituality, sometimes focusing my attention on the structure of ritual and forgetting the purpose behind it. Once, in a single sentence, Gurudev reminded me of the purpose of all spiritual practices.

Puja is a symbolic devotional ceremony offering light, incense, and other traditional elements to God and guru. One of the ashram sisters, a friend of mine, was performing puja often as a key part of her devotional practice. I was impressed with her reverence and dedication to it.

This same puja-sister was working outside the ashram at that time as a business consultant for corporations. One night in satsanga she shared with Gurudev about the difficulties she was facing in meshing her spiritual life and values with her service in the business world.

Gurudev smiled and said, "If you are not doing puja when you are sitting with those businessmen, then all your pujas are useless." She lit up, realizing the true meaning of puja as an acknowledgement and an honoring of the divine in all people. In that one simple statement, Gurudev reminded all of us of the essence behind the form of our devotional practices.

— *CHANDRAKANT*

190

drugs, or alcohol to escape, others use work or goals. But every addiction is an escape from reality.

Orientation to a goal is disorientation to yourself, your inner source, the sense of peace and contentment you are longing to find at the end of your striving. When you focus on a goal, your center moves from you to something outside you. As you run after your goal, you become less and less attuned to the very self whom the goal was created to take care of.

Again, your pursuit of goals has been based on a false sense that you are not enough as you are and on the belief that there is something you must do, someone you must become, to feel complete and at peace. We all want peace, but often we strive to get it by creating disturbances in the name of pursuing goals, thereby losing our attunement to our real needs and frustrating our longing to be at peace.

Once you lose your attunement to your inner self, you can't even evaluate the results of your pursuit of goals. Having lost touch with who you really are, you experience only frustration, as you are caught in a never-ending cycle of replacing one goal with another. Even if you achieve each goal, you still feel unhappy.

Why is that, Gurudev?

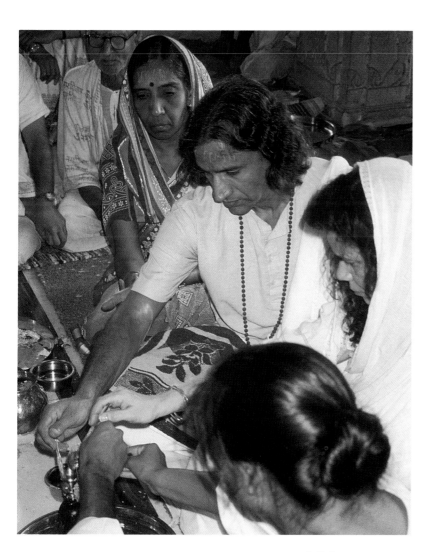

GURUDEV: One reason is that there's a basic lesson we can miss when we seek fulfillment and pleasure through goals, namely, that every experience comes with its opposite right behind it. So it's impossible to hold on to the peak feeling of happiness that comes with the achievement of a goal. Such is the balance and polarity of the universe, which is always at work.

The fun part of any experience—the part that is usually at the beginning —is eventually replaced by the painful part. As we get attached to the fun part, we want more of it and we gradually become addicted. What was once a great moment to be

191

Who's Serving Who?

There is a story in the book *Light From Guru to Disciple* that has always inspired me. In the story, Bapuji and Dadaji, his guru, are traveling on foot for several days. Bapuji grows more and more exhausted, but his pride prevents him from telling Dadaji how tired he feels. Finally Bapuji breaks down in tears, unable to go one step farther. Dadaji lovingly rubs his feet and takes care of him, while Bapuji, the grateful disciple, falls into a blissful sleep. I had a similar experience with Gurudev once.

Gurudev and I were going to St. Croix to look at property for a potential Kripalu center. The night before our departure I stayed up very late, packing and repacking for the trip with great excitement, thrilled to be traveling with and serving Gurudev. In the morning I showed up, drained and exhausted, for the three-hour drive to JFK airport.

Gurudev consciously and creatively uses every minute of time, including his travel time. He had asked Atma, an ashram writer, to come along for the ride to the airport to continue their work on a writing project while I drove.

As we prepared to leave, Atma was in the front seat and Gurudev was relaxing in the back, cozy with the pillows some thoughtful disciple had placed there for him. Feeling too tired to drive, I paused at her window and said quietly, "Atma, I'm exhausted. I would appreciate it if you drove to the airport." She thought for a moment and said, "But Yogesh, I can't drive and work with Gurudev at the same time."

Gurudev popped up from the back seat and said, "Oh, I'll drive."

"Oh, no, Gurudev," I responded. I wasn't prepared for that; I had only wanted Atma to drive. "You stay comfortable. We'll handle it." I felt that I, the disciple, was here to serve him, the guru.

"Don't be ridiculous," Gurudev said, getting out of the car. He opened the driver's door and slid behind the steering wheel. "You relax, Yogesh. Sit in the back."

Sheepishly I climbed into the back, lay down on the seat, and snuggled into Gurudev's pillows, wrapping his still warm blanket around me. I realized that Gurudev did not think a thing of driving to New York and discussing Atma's writing project while I rested.

Like the child who feels proud of helping Mom or Dad with a chore while he himself is the one truly being taken care of, the disciple thinks that he is performing some service to the guru. The truth is that the guru is always performing a great service to the disciple. Like the exhausted Bapuji, sleeping as his guru rubbed his feet, I relaxed gratefully into the warm softness of Gurudev's service to me. A small smile touched my lips as I fell into a deep, delicious sleep.

— *YOGESH*

experienced has now become an addiction that takes us out of the succeeding moments and actually becomes a source of pain.

It's not the pain that's bad, mind you; it's our wanting to avoid the pain. One of the meanings of the word "yoga" is the integration of the opposites inherent in this world of polarity through embracing the whole. To embrace the whole of any experience, you must accept both the fun and the painful parts of it equally, just as they show up. And, if you examine your life, you will see that often the painful times have created a new opening, a breakthrough into learning and growth that changes your life for the better.

As when a forest burns, it appears to be devastation, but then incredible new growth comes.

GURUDEV: Yes. There can be no breakthrough without breakdown in front of it.

If I'm using clay to mold a shape and I don't like the shape I'm making, I have to demolish that one before I can make another. I make the new shape by starting with the one that is in my hand, the one I don't like.

So let your life be as pliable as clay! Stay flexible to the inner, divine forces shaping you, rather than trying to hold onto the shape you feel secure in.

Walk the fine line between the passion of a goal-oriented businessperson and the detachment of a yogi. The key is to live for the purpose of accepting what the moment brings. With practice, you will get better and better at it.

Remember, if you keep your focus on how you *be*, not what you *do*, then whatever you do will bring fulfillment. Fulfillment will flow from your immersion in each moment, and you can carry out both your work and your life with joy and passion for everything you do. ◆

"ENJOY YOURSELF!"

The freedom and spontaneity with which you were chanting and dancing just now is a beautiful expression of your love. Such devotion is called "bhakti" and it is the nectar of spiritual life.

Bhakti provides a different dimension to open your heart so you can receive God's love. You cannot capture God's love through only the stark practice of being in witness consciousness. Bhakti provides a taste of a spiritual experience that is totally different from witnessing.

Sometimes you can become dry by being in the witness all the time. So, sing your heart out—jump up and down—enjoy yourself!

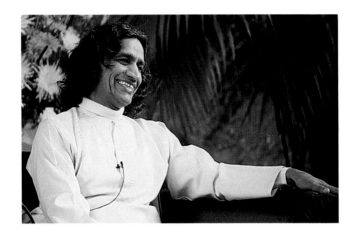

Sari Humor

Gurudev has very different relationships with his many disciples. He is a cosmic chameleon, adapting his personality and expression to meet those of each person he serves. I have a wacky sense of humor and use joking to create relationship and intimacy. Gurudev has noticed that about me and has always related to me with humor, the quickest way to my heart.

When I was a young disciple, I received some strange sari material from well-meaning friends in Minnesota, where winters are frigid and saris are few. The drapery-weight material was thick, dense cotton—not your average, lightweight, silky sari cloth. When I pleated the skirt, it billowed voluminously around my hips in an uncooperative lump.

One day, with my new sari material bundled smartly around me, I held the car door open for Gurudev as he arrived for satsanga. Glancing with surprise at my sari, he said to me, "You know, Vrajmala, you really should learn how to put on a sari properly." Although he said it gently, I was devastated and slunk away, grateful that nobody was around to hear. Gurudev asked his assistant to teach me how to wrap a sari, and she and I began lessons. But sari wrapping was not my forte.

The next week during satsanga, I went up front and with exaggerated drama told Gurudev about a conflict I was having with my roommate, which at that moment seemed to me an important, bordering on life-threatening problem. Sobbing and teary-eyed, I rambled on and on. When I was finished he said with a mischievous grin, "Vrajmala, why don't you stand up so we can see your sari?"

I stood up and my sari was a heap of white material chaotically lumped around my waist, my sari wrapping lessons gone to naught. Forgetting my emotional drama, I started to laugh. Gurudev joined in and soon the whole resident family was chortling with glee, the seriousness of my story broken. I felt such genuine acceptance for who I was from Gurudev and the family. Reaching me through humor, Gurudev loved me, showed his acceptance of me, and taught me to take my life less seriously.

— *VRAJMALA*

Bananas Foster

Gurudev has the extraordinary ability to be with what is present without judgement or self-criticism.

We were at the World Yoga Conference. Hundreds of yoga students from dozens of countries had come to hear the world's premier yogis, and Gurudev was one of the principal teachers. The conference was being held at Club Med in Zinal, Switzerland. It was lunch time, and Gurudev and I were sitting in the gorgeous dining room enjoying each other's company.

At one point, Gurudev got up and headed toward the dessert table. I twisted my neck, trying to see what he was doing. Minutes passed. Finally I saw him returning to the table, a broad smile on his face. He had six or seven tiny samples of luscious desserts. I shook my head with disbelief as my guru approached carrying such delights as chocolate cake and glorious-looking Danish pastry.

While I sat there boxed in by my concepts about diet—locked in my "thou shalt not's" about sugar and chocolate—I observed Gurudev's freedom. He routinely eats a very healthy diet, and he eats with consciousness and care. Yet, because he lives without concepts, Gurudev was able to enjoy himself spontaneously in that Club Med setting. He had no need to attach any significance or fear to the eating of desserts, even in the presence of students who might have concepts about how he should behave. He just ate the desserts with gusto.

I ended up joining Gurudev in having dessert, but without the gusto. Loaded down with inflexible dietary concepts, I ate worrying about how I would feel later. Meanwhile, in the center of the room, the chef began to make a flaming dessert called Bananas Foster, and Gurudev went to get a sample of that exotic creation also.

The postscript to this story is remarkable to me. The lecture that Gurudev gave directly after that lunch of dessert–samplings was brilliant. As I sat in the haze of my self-inflicted sugar hangover, I watched him teach with clarity and presence. Gurudev moved fully into the next event, leaving the desserts behind. He didn't miss a beat— not an instant of his life.

— *BRAHMANAND*

EXPERIENCE

Your experience is your experience is your experience. It is neither good nor bad. As soon as you label it, you've separated yourself from life and all the life-giving forces surrounding you. Reality is God. Embracing your experience, your reality, without judging it, leads you to higher consciousness. To experience life fully, without distortion, is to embrace God.

What Happened

As part of my training when I joined the ashram's editorial department, I attended a darshan with Gurudev with another writer who was working on a book with him. Gurudev was in wonderful form—a veritable fountain of ideas and inspiration. I was enthralled, and just sat soaking it all in.

Toward the end of the session, Gurudev talked about the alternative to expressing or suppressing strong feelings or desires: simply experiencing those feelings consciously.

My colleague hesitated a moment, then said, "Gurudev, I'm certainly an example of that teaching today. I've been sitting here with quite a lot of feelings because I expected to go over certain material for the book, and you were teaching on other subjects."

Gurudev responded, "You did very well, because you didn't express your feelings inappropriately or suppress them. You stayed with yourself."

"I don't know, " she answered, shaking her head. "This morning's session would have felt better for me if you had covered the specific material I need for this chapter."

"You're absolutely right," Gurudev agreed. "It would have been much better if I had kept to that topic. After all, you have a deadline to meet. It would have been much more efficient if I had spoken on that topic the entire morning." Then he shrugged and threw up his hands in a "what-can-you-do?" gesture, exclaiming with a smile, "but that isn't what happened!"

Since that day, I have used the phrase "but that isn't what happened" to remind myself to let go of my attachment to the way I think life should present itself to me and accept what it actually presents.

As Gurudev said on a different occasion: "Whenever we put our expectations before what is, we are putting the cart before the horse." With Gurudev's life as my example, I am definitely into dropping what I cart around as expectations in favor of riding the horse of reality!

— *BHAVANI*

Cappuccino

I'm a coffee drinker. I like it and I drink it, and I watch my mind judging that.

Gurudev was coming to spend a weekend at my house while he taught a seminar in the area and my coffee habit was a concern for me. "What if the smell offends him?" I thought. "Will he consider me a bad disciple because I drink it? Can I go without drinking coffee for two days?" On and on my mind went, creating stories about my relationship to coffee and to my guru.

On our first morning together we were downtown, and when lunchtime approached I decided to take Gurudev to my favorite Mexican restaurant. This restaurant has wonderful vegetarian bean burritos and also serves great iced cappuccino, which, by that point in the day, I was vividly tasting in my mind. It was definitely time for me to have some coffee. I took a breath and said to the waiter, "One iced cappuccino, please," still fearing Gurudev's reaction. The waiter brought out a tall glass filled with the frothy nectar and I began to sip it.

"What's that?" Gurudev asked.

I told him, "Gurudev, this is iced cappuccino, espresso coffee mixed with steamed milk. I enjoy coffee and I've spent hours worrying about what you might think of me because I still drink it."

Gurudev looked over at me with a beautiful smile and said, "Let's order one for me, too."

As usual, Gurudev was offering me an opportunity to accept myself fully. His graciousness touched me deeply as we sat there, my guru and I, sipping iced cappuccino together.

— *VASUDEV*

REALITY

Concepts cover reality,
distorting.

Consciousness unveils reality,
revealing.

Ego distorts;
consciousness
always clarifies.

Reality is relentless.

It follows behind every denial,
every avoidance,
until it is embraced
with open arms.

Let It Be What It Is

Let go of that which is gone.
Let go of that which is lost.
Let go of that which is not yet happening.
What has happened in the past and what will happen
in the future exist only in your mind.
What is happening now is the infinite caress of the universe.
To touch the eternal now and let it enfold you in its infinite love
is the essence of being in love.
What is happening now is the perfect outcome
of all you have been, and all you have done.
It is all here to teach you.
It is all here to love you.
It is all here to liberate you.
And it is all perfect.
Release that which is going out.
Embrace that which is coming in.
Leave alone that which has not yet come.
Want nothing, and embrace everything.
Relax into what is, and what is will take care of you.
Let it be what it is.

Appendix: about Kripalu Yoga Fellowship and Kripalu Center

Kripalu Yoga Fellowship is a nonprofit religious and educational organization created by Gurudev in 1974 to serve as the umbrella for all the different manifestations of the Kripalu work.

Foremost among those is the Kripalu Center for Yoga and Health, a spiritual community and world-renowned educational facility for yoga and holistic health, located in the Berkshire hills of western Massachusetts. Open year-round, the Center offers programs and individual health services that promote the integration of body, mind, and spirit through authentic yogic disciplines combined with contemporary approaches to personal growth. The combination provides not just intellectual understanding, but first-hand experiences that lead to radiant well-being and a greater sense of aliveness for more than fifteen thousand guests each year.

The Center's programs range in length from a day to a month and focus on spiritual attunement, health and fitness, and professional training. The spiritual attunement programs teach participants to use yoga, meditation, selfless service, conscious relationships, and other transformational self-discovery techniques to create lives of fulfilled human potential. The health and fitness programs emphasize the body as temple of the spirit, using yoga, exercise, healthy diet, fasting, and stress management for holistic health. The certification programs train participants to be professional yoga teachers, bodyworkers, and holistic health educators.

Center guests also have the option of an unstructured schedule with as much variety and activity as desired. Daily classes in yoga, meditation, and aerobic dance are available to everyone, as are the Center's extensive facilities that include saunas and whirlpools, and the beautiful estate grounds that feature rolling lawns, miles of walking trails through quiet woods, and a private lakefront. Individual health services provided to guests and the general public include sessions in bodywork, energy balancing, Shiatsu, and reflexology.

The Center offers a residential program for those who wish to learn and practice a yogic lifestyle as a member of the Kripalu staff, starting with a three-month work/study program. Residents receive comprehensive training in the same spiritual and health techniques taught in guest programs, and they have the added advantage of learning to apply those techniques as a way of life in the unique environment created by the presence of a yoga master and a community of dedicated spiritual seekers. Living a simple ashram lifestyle in a contemporary setting, the residents are able to devote their lives to their spiritual advancement

through the study of yoga and scriptures and a vigorous lifestyle of selfless service. The children of the community attend a home school program that provides an education designed to nurture and integrate body, mind, and spirit.

More than five hundred Kripalu Center residents, having received in-depth training in the Kripalu lifestyle, have returned to the world at large to offer their skills to their local communities as yoga teachers, holistic health practitioners, and support group leaders, in addition to serving in their primary professions. Similarly, in

Sumneytown, Pennsylvania—the site of the original Kripalu ashram—a new type of Kripalu community is currently being created, one made up of families and individuals who share the practice of a yogic lifestyle while maintaining their involvement in the world through their jobs and professions.

In addition to Kripalu Center, Kripalu Yoga Fellowship currently encompasses a network of over one thousand yoga teachers, over four hundred holistic health practitioners and bodyworkers, and over one hundred Kripalu support groups and centers across the U.S. and fifteen other countries. Over 125,000 subscribers receive *The Kripalu Experience*, the magazine that contains articles by Gurudev and the latest information about Kripalu programs.

In India, the motherland of yoga as well as of Bapuji and Gurudev, Kripalu Yoga Fellowship supports the humanitarian and spiritual work begun by Bapuji by contributing to the two ashrams he founded. The spiritual director of those ashrams is Gurudev's guru-brother, Swami Shri Rajarshi Muni, an eminent sage and author and one of Bapuji's closest disciples, who in his sadhana

is following in Bapuji's footsteps. In addition, the Fellowship supports various educational and humanitarian projects in the state of Gujarat.

Looking toward the future, the Fellowship recently acquired another property—a fully equipped health facility near the Lenox center—with plans to extend the Kripalu work into the field of corporate wellness training.

Perhaps the best picture of Kripalu's work can be drawn from the accounts of visitors, including journalists, who have described their first-time experiences of the Center and Gurudev.

In the best of all possible worlds, people would love and respect each other. They would recognize the grace and beauty in all people. They would be truly equal and view each other without judgement or criticism. In the best of all possible worlds, the human being would rise to the highest level of pure thought and integrity. Everyone would trust. The body would be the human temple and value would be placed on its care and maintenance. There would be complete satisfaction. An atmosphere of peace and harmony would reign.

Rubbish, you say? Well, I'm here to let you know that it does exist. Smack in the middle of a world filled with mad marauders, highjackers, terrorists, thrill-seekers, and product-happy yuppies, the Kripalu Center offers a slice of life at its potential optimum.

Merna Popper
Women's News

Kripalu is not a spa, or at least, it doesn't call itself one. It is a nonprofit yoga and meditation center that draws people seeking a more spiritual life. But like a spa, Kripalu offers a chance to learn something new, to regenerate. . . .

Time takes on a different quality in such a quiet environment. Even the rule that guests wear modest clothing (sweat suits instead of leotards, for example) contributes to a feeling of calm and purity. A day seemed like a week. There was no television, no radio, no need to talk to anyone. . . . [A]t Kripalu, there isn't the expectation of conversation. Being naturally reserved, I simply stopped speaking for two days. . . .

By the end of my second day, I had lost all desire for chocolate, my one true addiction. Time had slowed to almost nothing. I was calm. I was relaxed. And, although I am sometimes embarrassingly resistant to the whole idea of a spiritual path, I could see how life in this community could be rich. On the final morning, I picked up my bowl of cornflakes and headed for my customary solitary seat in the dining room. Only then did I realize that absolutely no one was talking. Every pair of eyes was raised to the large windows, looking with awe at the falling snow. It was a genuinely transcendent moment.

Trish Hall
New York Times

From the moment visitors enter the double glass doors of Kripalu's main building, many sense an atmosphere of peace and tranquility. The attitude of the staff at the front desk goes beyond a learned marketing skill. All of Kripalu's staff believe their spiritual growth is enhanced by serving others. And serve they do, with a care—and some would say a love—not found in ordinary spas or getaways.

Ruth Mason
Baltimore Jewish Times

Kripalu is about as far removed as you can get from Hare Krishna cults, aberrated Buddhist and Tantric groups given to sex orgies, and phony-baloney "Oriental" groups big on peacock feathers and incense. The ambience here for programs of yoga, self-discovery, relaxing, unwinding, and unfolding draws as much on Christian-Judeo themes as it does on the practice of pranayama . . .

Because Kripalu is a nonprofit organization, costs are kept down, and prices are refreshingly affordable. At these prices, people don't mind being asked to bring their own blanket or mat for yoga exercises, or make their own bed. Summer, winter, spring, or autumn, Kripalu is a unique environment for personal development, greater health, and lasting take-home benefits.

Theodore B. Van Itallie, M.D., and Leila Hadley
The Best Spas

Kripalu staff members don't just teach techniques for better health. They provide a supportive environment in which people can make the change to a more healthful life-style—one that they themselves have tried, tested, and lived. . . .Visitors learn how to improve their work, their relationships, and their level of self-fulfillment. And they learn to laugh about and release their fears.

Corrine McLaughlin
Yoga Journal

Kripalu is indeed unique—vibrant, instructive, inspiring. The staff is a very impressive group—healthy, cheerful, and friendly . . . A haven and school for all who seek physical, mental, and spiritual well-being, Kripalu is an inspiring example of the potentialities of life.
Ronald Kotzch
East West Journal

Since the passing of my guru Bishnu Ghosh, I have met many yogis all over the world purporting to possess true yogic spirit. Sadly, none of them came close to joining my guru in my heart.

From the instant of my first meeting with Yogi Amrit Desai, I experienced a deep spiritual connection to him. The sort of connection one can only have with another human being, if that being possesses a higher level of consciousness.

This first deep impression was further validated when at his invitation I spent a week at the Kripalu Yoga Ashram. Only a man in possession of a pure yogic spirit can transmit it to others. Guruji has created a place where his disciples are experiencing and expressing an intense joy of life. A place where spirituality, individuality and practicality have merged in a conscious and harmonic life experience.
Bikram Choudhury
Founder-Director, Yoga College of India

Unfortunately, the "modern Guru" usually sets himself on such a high pedestal, that none but the "chosen few" can approach him . . . The "masses" are kept at bay, and are given only rare "Darshan" or glimpses of the "holy Master." Not so Yogiraj Amrit Desai—one of his greatest qualities as we here at Ananda Ashram see it is his accessibility to his disciples and followers— he lives amongst his students, he lives with them, and he teaches them by his own example. This close interaction between Guru and Chela is rare in Yoga organizations today, in fact, nearly non-existent. How ironic, since this "mouth to ear" tradition of Guruship here in India has always been the close interaction, the intimate relationship between Guru and disciple.
Smt. Meenakshi Devi
Yoga Life

Glossary of Sanskrit Terms

arati—a ceremony of light honoring the divine light within each of us

asanas—hatha yoga postures; third limb of classical yoga

ashram—a spiritual community or retreat; usually the home of a spiritual master

Bapuji—"dear Father"; the name affectionately given to Gurudev's guru, Swami Shri Kripalvanandji

brahmacharya—"actions that lead to brahman," or God; usually refers to the practice of celibacy and moderation of all the senses

Dadaji—"dear Grandfather"; the familiar name given to the guru of Bapuji

darshan—a meeting or audience with a spiritual master

dharma—duty; the precepts of divine law or truth

diksha—inititation

guru—"dispeller of darkness"; a spiritual master

Guru Purnima—an annual celebration in honor of the guru

Gurudev—"beloved teacher"; a respectful way of addressing one's guru

karma—action; usually refers to the universal law of action and reaction, cause and effect

karma yoga—the yoga of action or selfless service

Kripalu—"the compassionate or merciful one"; the name of Gurudev's guru, for whom the Kripalu work is named

kriya—a yogic action or technique performed for physical, emotional, or mental purification; may occur spontaneously during spiritual practices

kundalini—a powerful evolutionary energy lying dormant at the base of the spine; usually awakened only through intense spiritual practice

Kundalini Yoga—a scientific branch of yoga designed to activate the energy of kundalini and channel it creatively for higher spiritual consciousness

mantra—sacred words or sounds that can be repeated as a meditation technique to still the mind

prana—the vital life force

pranayama—control of the vital life force; practices for controlling the breath; fourth limb of classical yoga

puja—a ceremony of love and reverence involving offerings of incense, flowers, water, and light

sadhak—a spiritual aspirant; a practitioner of yoga

sadhana—spiritual practices

samadhi—the experience of oneness with God

sanatana dharma—the ancient path or religion of eternal truth, promoting ethical and moral behavior, love for family, and service to humanity

satsanga—a spiritual gathering, often in the presence of the guru

seva—selfless service

shakti—the creative, transformative, spiritual energy within man

shaktipat—the transmission of spiritual energy from guru to disciple

shastras—ancient Indian scriptures outlining ways to the realization of truth

tapas—spiritual practices that purify the mind, emotions, and body; the spiritual fire that burns the aspirant's impurities

tapascharya—willful practice of tapas

yoga—union; self-integration and realization; the merging of the individual consciousness with the universal energy (God)

213